ALSO BY GARY JOHN BISHOP

Unfu*k Yourself

STOP
DOING THAT
SH*T

End Self-Sabotage and
Demand Your Life Back

GARY JOHN BISHOP

HarperOne
An Imprint of HarperCollins*Publishers*

HarperOne

HarperCollins books may be purchased for educational, business, or sales promotional use. For information, please email the Special Markets Department at SPsales@harpercollins.com.

FIRST EDITION

Designed by Terry McGrath

Library of Congress Cataloging-in-Publication Data

Names: Bishop, Gary John, author.
Title: Stop doing that sh*t : end self-sabotage and demand your
  life back / Gary John Bishop.
Other titles: Stop doing that shit
Description: San Francisco : HarperOne, 2019.
Identifiers: LCCN 2019005027 | ISBN 9780062950147 (paperback) |
  ISBN 9780062934789 (hardcover) | ISBN 9780062871848 (hardcover) |
  ISBN 9780062945884 (trade PB) | ISBN 9780062871855 (e-book)
Subjects: LCSH: Self-actualization (Psychology) | Motivation
  (Psychology) | BISAC: SELF-HELP / Personal Growth / Success. |
  BUSINESS & ECONOMICS / Motivational. | SELF-HELP / Personal
  Growth / Happiness.
Classification: LCC BF637.S4 B537 2019 | DDC 158.1–dc23 LC
  record available at https://lccn.loc.gov/2019005027

22 23 24 25 26 LBC 6 5 4 3 2

I dedicate this book to the helpless and hopeless, the frustrated and defeated: today is a day when it can all begin anew. I don't care about your past, and you shouldn't either.

Thanks to my beautiful wife and inspiring sons, without whom I could never be the man I have become. Through your generosity and love, we are a family committed to making a difference in this world.

Contents

01

Here's the Rub

In your day-to-day life you are, for the most part, on autopilot.

Someone once asked me, "What's at the core of every human being?"

"Bullshit," I replied.

There were a few nervy moments of shoe-gazing silence followed by a gust of swirly, disjointed questions to cover the unease.

Apparently, they were expecting some new-age, metaphysical answer about untethered spirit or essence of ancient forests or particles of distant stardust sprinkled with fairy juice. But my response was (and is) unequivocal. In my experience of people (yes, I'm people too, as are you), if you set aside all of the positivity and hope, there is quite clearly a whole other animal lurking below the surface, a *conversational* bullshit if you like, something not quite as empowering or comforting as we'd all like to believe. Not evil or nefarious but rather something more akin to cynical, constraining, repetitive, and ultimately unfulfilling.

The kind of stuff that undermines a life. Sabotages it, to be precise.

This wee book is my take on finally uncovering and transforming your bullshit. The kind that constantly sabotages your life.

So, if you're tired, overwhelmed, overworked, underloved, stopped, paused, bored, broke, too anxious, too analytical, lacking confidence, uninspired, disconnected, on the wrong path, headed in the wrong direction, bottomed out, mired in the past, worried about the future, disappointed, afraid, untrusting, unforgiving, suspicious, angry, frustrated, or just plain stuck in a cycle, I'm your guy and these are your pages.

No, really, they're yours. Don't just read them, use them.

Let's get to the blackened heart of that bullshit, then root it out.

———————

In my last book, *Unfu*k Yourself: Get Out of Your Head and Into Your Life*, I wrote about the constant internal chatter that we all deal with. The noise of opinion, judgment, reasons, fears, and excuses that rattle around in our heads every moment of every day. Sometimes it's loud, sometimes it's quiet, but nonetheless, it's always there. Your self-talk is the locker room of your life. Where everything is strategized and worked out. Where your plans for yourself live and die.

Most of these plans never see the light of day. Especially the good stuff, the dreams. You kill them where they rise. In your head.

People are little more than a living conversation, both internal and spoken. A dialogue in a body. A skin-and-bone bag that talks, and it talks about everything, and the limit of that talk is the limit of that life. Period.

In short, you are what you talk about, or rather you are the *nature* of what you talk about. If, for you, life is too much, it really *is* too much! The confusion is that you think life is a certain way and you are just reporting on what you are seeing. But that's actually backward. The reality is, you create your experience of life in your self-talk and then act accordingly. And you're doing it all the time. You're never (like never, ever) acting upon life itself. What you are acting on is your *opinion* of life. That's why it's such a different experience for each of us.

Life just *is*. What you call it is up to you. Bear in mind you'll have to live with your call. And you do.

This isn't something new either.

Philosophers such as Hans-Georg Gadamer, Edmund Husserl, and Martin Heidegger explored the importance of language and how it molds our as-lived experience of absolutely everything. Those feelings you have (or lack thereof) are constituted in your language. Your talk is your life, and we see it most glaringly in your regular little sashays into the world of self-sabotage.

This may require a bit of radical thinking on your part, but in a very real sense, your emotions and your conversations are in a constant tango with each other, swaying and swooping through life. As a society we have become increasingly addicted to changing our emotions—to feel happier, more confident, more whatever—and all without addressing what is enlivening those states. It's not the sucky life you seemingly have but your dialogue *about* your life that has you by the throat, and the vast majority of that dialogue is blissfully unnoticed and therefore unexplored by you. It's running in the background.

This book takes the work we started in *Unfu*k Yourself* to the next level. We're out to finally uncover *your* personal brand of self-talk and discover why it remains the source of all that's currently shitty in your life. In the day-to-day living of our lives, we mostly just experience the moods and emotions of our internal chatter without doing the work to determine what it's *really* saying. So, if you've ever wanted to know why you talk to yourself in the way you do and, more specifically, what it is that drives that talk . . . read on.

Before you start to think I'm slipping into another "positive thoughts" cliché, let's get something clear. There's a reason simply changing your self-talk to "I'm good enough" or "I'm smart enough" or "I am loved" or "I can do it" to overcome the negative BS doesn't quite work for everyone.

The problem with that approach is that it doesn't address the muck. You just can't *be* one way to overcome another way that you don't like. You can't short-circuit the process. It's the emotional equivalent of sweeping the dead cockroaches under the rug before your friends arrive. Sure, it all looks good, but in your heart of hearts you know the dead cockroaches are still there. It's like that in our minds— when we sweep the negative emotion under our mental rug, deep down we still know *something else*. Something more akin to the truth. It's like lying to yourself but you just don't believe the lie. A con game.

We're using these pages to get under that rug. To reveal those hidden emotional cockroaches and free you up, to let you authentically *be* rather than pretend to *be*. You can, of course, shift your emotional state by *doing*, a process I covered in my first book, but the common denominator in all of this is language.

The way we work is that we can only ever *be* one way at a time. You can't be angry *and* loving simultaneously in a single moment. It's one or the other. You can't be forgiving *and* resentful or indifferent *and* sad. At any moment in time, you're always *being* one way and ONLY one way.

———————

Before we dive in, a few people commented that my last book didn't say much about me, so I'm rectifying that right here and now.

I'm Scottish. Full-on accent, with a penchant for kilts and crappy weather.

I love empowering people. My life's work is to give people something that might allow them to change their lives for the better. I don't do that by telling you you're awesome or that one day your ship will come in or that everything happens for a reason or any other kind of modern, new-agey schtick that some people have come to adopt.

I give it to you straight. Right between the eyeballs. You are the problem, and you are the solution!

(As a related aside, someone once told me I'm not everyone's cup of tea. "Tea isn't everyone's cup of tea either" was my response.)

I'm also not arrogant enough to think I could solve a conundrum that has perplexed philosophers, scholars, scientists, and great minds as far back as we (or at least I) can trace. My single intention is to make a difference with one person. You. That's it. If you're reading this and focusing on how it applies to your spouse, your dad, your boss, your cousin, or your ex, you're completely missing the point.

This book is *for* you and *about* you.

That's it.

So, what is this book?

For starters, this book is a short, intense jolt to your way of thinking. I'm not out to give you all the answers here. Your answers will come from *you*. They always do. This is more like a catalyst, providing questions and ways of looking at things that will spark something in you and cause you to take on your life in a new way.

Inspiration, motivation, passion, and whatever else you are looking for in your life is on you. That has been the case in the past, it is the case in the present, and it will be the case in the future.

A big part of living the life you want is taking ownership of your choices, now and in the future. This book is more like a voyage of self-discovery, of thinking about and uncovering and ultimately revealing your true nature. When you finally understand where you are coming from, you are giving yourself a greater shot at changing how your life will go.

I approach this book from my own little brand of "urban philosophy." I say "philosophy" because that's just what this is, a view, an angle on what it is to be alive, to be a human being and attempt to make our way through the complexity, fear, and struggle to some sort of consistent happiness and success. I use the word "urban" because the greatest lessons of my life were learned in the black-and-white streets of my Glaswegian childhood, where the rules were simple and the consequences clinical.

This is a model that I created. I looked at many different disciplines and approaches, studied a number of philosophers, took what made sense to me, and started to dig. I've used this model with my clients and found that when they put in the work, when they get down to that true, driving nature of theirs, monumental change really is possible. What I've come up with is a way for you to look at your own wiring, to understand your self-sabotage so that you have real pathways to spring free from the morass of what you have become and experience the freedom to take yourself on once and for all. To do that, you might have to push through some initial confusion and disagreement. That's okay. Be aware that much of what I say here might be counterintuitive to the way you currently see yourself. Eh . . . that's kinda the point.

This book has curse words in it, just like the last one, and most likely the next one too. I like curse words. They sprinkle much-needed life into the otherwise jaded landscape of our everyday talk. If you can't handle a few choice expletives in life, well, I was going to say "Put this book down," but to hell with it, you need what I'm about to say more than most. Buckle in and read on.

Let my intention be clear: I'm out to give you knowledge—real, juicy, life-changing knowledge— that you can use to think and think and think your way out of this cluster of confusion and self-defeating behavior you've gotten yourself into.

When I say "think," I'm not talking about the kind of gummy pondering/wondering/thought-ing you do in the drift of your daily life while pumping gas or making your favorite banana-bacon sandwich (really?), but rather a deliberate and intentional engagement with an idea. Real thinking is what can happen when your existing paradigm (all the stuff you know) gets challenged and interrupted.

This thinking thing is *not* easy. It's the kind of mental stretching required when you are quite literally *forced* to consider something else, something you hadn't considered or at best partially considered, and then do the work to connect it to your life. Thinking is an interruption. Real breakthroughs become available in your life when you interrupt yourself and your automatic responses to whatever life presents you with.

The German philosopher Martin Heidegger once wrote: "The most thought-provoking thing in our thought-provoking time is that we are still not thinking."

You don't think. There. I said it.

I'm not attempting to make you choke on the next hearty quaff of that iced venti half-caff sugar-free skinny cinnamon dolce soy latte that you're currently sucking down like a freshly emptied Dyson on full throttle. We spend very little time doing the actual thinking that will inspire new lives for ourselves, and no, scrolling through quotes on Instagram doesn't count as thinking.

The thinking you do throughout this book will help you to make sense of yourself.

What you do with that? That's up to you, but I wouldn't advise just sitting there with it. You could, oh,

I don't know, change your freaking life or something.

But it's not a given. This is your life, and it needs work. You could spend your time challenging what I am proposing, or you could spend your time challenging yourself with what I am proposing. Each will produce a different outcome. It's pretty damn obvious which one could lead you to change your life and which one will leave you spinning your wheels.

It starts by waking up.

In your day-to-day life you are, for the most part, on autopilot. It's why you miss the exit on your way to or from work, why you put on your pants, shoes, or jacket the same way every time, brush your teeth the way you do, and generally just get life done. Automatically.

You're not up on your toes, awake to your potential. You're not alive to what it is that truly lights you up or engaged with the kind of life-changing stuff that will make this all worthwhile.

What you think is "awake" is actually asleep. You might wake up near the end of this existence, but that will probably be far too late for you. Wake up to *that*, at least.

While you read this, there might be some occasions when you'll need to take a chain-breaking leap from the anchor of what you currently believe. It's fine, you won't die. Dare yourself to jump.

Here's a little pointer. From time to time you might want to wake up to how you are engaging with this book. Check in with how you're doing. I recommend breaking this process up into sections to give yourself time to percolate with what I'm proposing, take notes, highlight what you need, and come up for the occasional gulp of air. We are dealing with your propensity for self-sabotage, after all. We won't be frolicking through the abundant, joyous fields of your heart's desire in these pages. More like wading our way through decades of your unwanted strife, lack of fulfillment, and constant sabotaging of all that is good in your life!

This might not be comfortable for you.

Some of you might find what seems like a lot of bad news in these pages.

Oh well.

There are no unicorns or states of euphoria or, hell, not even a particularly sympathetic ear. There's a time and a place for all that stuff. This is not the time or the place, that's all. However, I do have a promise for you. If you hang in there until the end, do the thinking, uncover your subconscious motivations, and apply the ideas and principles, you'll make more sense to yourself than you ever have, *and* you'll have what you need to finally demand your life back.

It's possible to interrupt the cycle of self-sabotage. Let's get to it, shall we?

02

A Life of Sabotage

There's nothing quite so damaging as the human desire to be right.

When I talk about self-sabotage, what do I mean specifically? *Merriam-Webster's Collegiate Dictionary* defines "sabotage" as

> *"destructive or obstructive action carried on by a civilian or enemy agent to hinder a nation's war effort" or*
> *"a: an act or process tending to hamper or hurt b: deliberate subversion."*

But in this case, sabotage isn't apparently committed by an "enemy agent"—or is it? Maybe the enemy agent is you yourself.

This is sabotage committed by us, against ourselves, and it can subvert just about everything good in our lives.

It is a deliberate subversion, though. Completely deliberate.

You can probably think of some examples of self-sabotage by taking a look at the people who have come and gone through the musty hallways of your life.

It's always much easier to measure the decline of others than your own.

It could be an uncle who struggled with drug or alcohol addiction, stuck in a cycle of self-destruction he couldn't seem to break free from. Or maybe it's an old friend who lost their savings, their house, and even their family to compulsive gambling and the burden of debt.

Then there's the sibling who binges on crappy food until their weight is hopelessly out of control and even their life is now in very real danger. Or the nephew who still lives with Mom and Dad in his twenties, thirties, or forties, shunning real-world independence, accomplishment, and growth and choosing a digital escape of video game conquests and internet porn. Hell, some of this might be what you're dealing with yourself. These are all obvious examples of self-sabotage.

But what about the *less* obvious examples? Maybe you're reading this and thinking you're not *that* badly affected. Sure, you have your hang-ups and your vices. You'd like to achieve more at work or find a good partner or shave a smidgen of excess living off that tiny corner of your left ankle (okay, it's a spongy layer of fat clinging onto your gut like a panicky squid, but I'm being nice here). You have goals of reading more, watching less TV, or getting in better shape. But your behavior isn't nearly as self-destructive as in these examples . . . right?

But here's the thing. The sabotage I'm talking about isn't limited to those blatantly obvious examples. It's also something that happens in lots of little ways throughout the day. It's something we all do, and we're doing it pretty much all the time.

It can be something as simple as constantly hitting that snooze button in the morning, or the tendency to show up a little late to places you're scheduled to be. Not so late that it becomes a major problem, but you still find yourself rushing out the door as you shove your feet into your untied shoes and arriving five or ten minutes later than you'd like. Sometimes it looks like skipping breakfast and settling instead for a candy bar. Or maybe you're one of those people who chronically procrastinate but always manage to get things done at the last moment, so you don't think too much of it. Living on the edge, huh?

How's that working out for you?

There are probably examples in your relationships too. Think about the times when you argue over nothing, hold onto grudges too long, hide or lie about your emotions, judge yourself or others too harshly, or just don't call your mom or dad or friends as much as you should. Surely that's not self-sabotage?

The straight of it is, these are all actions that diminish relationships over time. They eat away at and destabilize healthy connections with the people we care most about. Sometimes to the point where we no longer care about them.

We become disconnected from the people we care about. And we feel justified. Oh boy, are we justified. There's nothing quite so damaging as the human desire to be right.

How can that NOT be an act of self-sabotage?

On the other end of the spectrum are the people who will cheat on or break up with their partner on a whim as a convoluted way of protecting themselves from being hurt in the future. Other people will become obsessively jealous over imagined affairs, creating discontent and disconnect so that there's no relatedness left. You might be someone who has done this. How did that turn out for you? There is such a thing as a self-fulfilling prophecy, even if it's not as mysterious or glamorous as we sometimes read about. Sometimes it just looks like imploding our relationships.

With regard to our health, self-sabotage can manifest itself in the ways we eat all the wrong stuff at all the wrong times, how we put off our exercise plans or use the excuse of getting caught up in the mundane details of our daily lives to explain our lack of action. We might give ourselves excuses to have "just one" cigarette or glass of wine or slice of cheesecake (which, of course, turns into more), skip doctor's visits and checkups, or just not pay enough attention to our body and what it's telling us.

Again, these aren't extreme examples. They're often subtle, so we don't even realize what we're doing or why we're doing it. Even if we do realize these actions are a problem, we don't understand that they're part of a larger pattern, a pattern that's carrying us in a predictable direction. The kind of pattern that keeps you perpetually weaving the life you currently have.

Skipping one little dentist's appointment or having one extra piece of chocolate cake isn't a big deal, right? Eh . . . wrong. What if that's part of a bigger plan? One that you're not keyed into, at least consciously.

You see, this self-sabotage thing is a product of something larger, and it's affecting every part of your life.

There's a reason why so few make it out of the trap of their own mind. The trap all too often seems to be just fine from day to day.

Step back a step or twenty and, eh, not so much.

It's little wonder that those big dreams of yours seem nigh impossible, given how challenging you've made it just to get out of bed in the morning. I mean, really? On one hand you talk about wanting to be an author or a business owner or going back to school, while at the same time you've reduced your life's potential to the lofty aim of getting up at the first alarm buzz or fighting the meaningless battle of prizing yourself away from your cell phone a little more often.

But ask yourself, if you really wanted to advance in your career, why would you be giving all of your attention to crappy little problems like not being able to get up in the morning? Why are you getting wrapped up in petty no-difference crap rather than the kinds of issues and actions that are going to move mountains, that are going to authentically engage you with real progress, real accomplishment, and real purpose?

If you really wanted to have a great love in your life, why in hell would you keep nitpicking your relationship to death until that connection decays right in front of your eyes? If you really wanted to get healthier or lose weight, why would you keep screwing around in such ordinary and uninspiring ways when it comes to making the changes you *say* you want to make?

> *You just can't keep responding in ordinary ways if you are truly out to live an extraordinary life.*

There has to be a potent demand on yourself to rise, to reach for greatness when compelled to take your typical low-road route, and there's no magic potion for that demand.

It's not a feeling or an attitude. It's more like a sick-of-your-own-nonsense approach to certain areas of life. If that deflates you, look again. It needs to enliven and inspire you.

Telling yourself the truth is rarely easy, but it's a surefire way to free yourself from your own subconscious self-sabotage trap. What makes self-reflection challenging is that you're both the con artist and the one being conned.

You see, we chalk the problems of our lives up to one of two things: either we believe there's a failure in our character or we blame our problems on external factors. We think it's just a matter of trying harder or getting lucky or knowing more. We think we just didn't start the right business, meet the right person, or find the right diet.

In reality, what we consciously think we want isn't lined up with what we are actually driven to do in the depths of our subconscious.

In Marcus Aurelius's personal writings to himself, which later became the famous philosophical work *Meditations*, he noted that

> *"The soul becomes dyed with the color of its thoughts."*

In our modern age, our soul is a tie-dyed fabric of all the thoughts and impressions and dreams we've had or have been given since we were babies. In the same way the dye seeps into the fabric, these thoughts are deeply embedded in our mind, in our subconscious.

And it's all too often not the color we want it to be.

That color you've dyed your soul, that set of invisible rules that have been embedded in the back of your mind, in your subconscious, is what determines your path through this life. It's not your determination, not your circumstances, and most definitely not your luck.

Luck is for those who cannot define their success, and if you cannot clearly define it, you will most likely never be able to repeat it.

THE THREE SABOTEURS—
AN INTRODUCTION

If you want to start doing something about your not-so-private little head game of self-sabotage, you'll need to first systematically uncover and then go about interrupting the conversations you have with yourself. Not the surface thoughts, but rather the repetitive, profoundly deep and dark internal dialogues that rattle around in your mental cage and guide your every thought and emotion. The stuff under the rug.

This will allow you to finally see your "three saboteurs," three simple internal statements that do real and lasting damage to you and your life. The three saboteurs are the fundamental conclusions you have come to about yourself, the other people in your life, and life itself. I know you might find it hard to believe that your entire existence is unraveling because of three simple internal statements, but it is, and in these pages I'll help you uncover not only why this is happening but also what your unique statements are.

How did you end up with your three saboteurs? We'll get to that. How do they impact your life (beyond the obvious)? We'll get to that too. How do you get yourself out of this crap? Oh, we'll get to that one, trust me.

For those of you who "Why? Why? Why?" the hell out of life, I have some answers for you too, although that incessant search for the answer is in many ways why the question is never satisfied.

Why? Oh, puhleeeeease!

I am out to unveil the inner workings of what makes you sabotage. We'll start at the beginning of your life and work our way to the very point of the spear. Today. In the first few chapters, we set the stage for why human beings would even have a propensity for sabotage in the first place, but it's safe to say your penchant for messing with your life didn't happen in a vacuum. Certain things had to happen in your life, in a particular sequence, some of which are common to all human beings, some that are unique to you. We'll uncover what these are for you.

This will take some work, and as you move through the chapters you might find yourself wiped out or in a state of confusion or fear. That's fine. The important thing is that you do not check out. Push through. On the other side of that state is a life you've always wanted to get to but somehow never could. Really.

I'm drawing a line in the sand with you right here.

You might discover that the effort you put into these pages is commensurate with the effort you have put into your life. That statement alone could change a life. Or not.

Get your head out of the sand (or your navel or wherever you currently have it buried) and *make* whatever you are reading here make a difference for you. You can do *that* at least.

> "Without ambition one starts nothing. Without work one finishes nothing. The prize will not be sent to you. You have to win it."
> —Ralph Waldo Emerson

Okay, champ, let's get rolling.

03

The Question

*That's what
we call a life.
Wanting new;
addicted to
the familiar.*

The idea for this book began with my asking myself a simple question.

Why?

Why is *my* life the way it is?

When I looked at my life I could see it was, in certain areas, headed in a direction that I wasn't particularly happy with. It seemed that regardless of the approach, there was always an inevitability about some areas of my life. My pillowy stomach. My finances. Certain relationships. I mean, damn, I've done TONS of growth work over the years and STILL my bank account gets overdrawn? Where's *my* Tony Robbins private helicopter/jet/submarine, for the love of God?

How come I've never *really* made a difference with these areas of my life? It's not as if I can't earn money, but how the hell have I seemingly always struggled so much to build it? It's not as if I don't know how to get my body in shape, but why is it always so temporary? No matter how much I tried, I would continually go in these cycles of winning, losing, winning, losing, and at the end of it all, wind up right back where I started. There have even been times when I was actually further *behind* after that real-life yo-yo!

It made no difference that I knew I kept getting into the same cycle and making the same mistakes. Like you, I'm not a freaking idiot! I can see what's wrong! However, no matter how hard I tried, it was as·if I would eventually be compelled to keep doing the same stuff I had always done, and I was apparently powerless to stop it! What the . . . ? I knew what I *wanted* to do, but I kept getting snagged by the hook of doing things the same way, going back to old and bankrupt and destructive behaviors.

You might want to take a breath here and ponder a couple of questions for yourself. Why do you do what you do? Again, go beyond the usual answer you give yourself. Think. If you keep living this way, where is it all headed? I mean *really* headed? Not some wispy concept of your future but rather a down-in-the-dirt look at where your current actions are leading you. Well? You might find those questions tough to answer, but this is the kind of digging that will release you from your trap of sabotage.

Earlier, I pointed out that self-sabotage isn't always the big, extreme things we do to screw up our lives. It's important to understand that there are millions of tiny ways we are sabotaging our lives every day. You have to see there's a problem before you can do anything about it. But it's important to understand that self-sabotage can also lead to very destructive behaviors. It shatters marriages, fractures families, turns people to hard drugs, alcohol, gambling and sex addictions, infidelity, and all kinds of toxic behaviors that trash an otherwise decent life.

When it comes down to it, no one can seriously fuck up your life quite as magnificently as you can. And you do.

In my career as a personal development guy, it's my job to help people have insights that empower them to make significant change in their lives. I've seen how very common it is for people to get stuck in cycles of behavior that, in the cold light of day, seem to be in complete opposition to what they say they want. Men and women the world over are trapped in a myopic stream of self-talk and patterns of behavior that keep them spinning in an all-too-predictable life.

Regardless of the number of times it seems life is on track, it always eventually seems to go off.

We are all building things only to burn them right back down. And we're tired of it.

YOU'RE NOT A CATEGORY

In looking for a way to get our lives back on track, I read somewhere that what we need is "willpower" or "discipline" or some other generic term (don't even get me started on "mental strength" . . . ugh) that serves only to help us explain to ourselves the lack of real change in our lives.

These terms are absolutely useless. They make zero difference!

What is "willpower," anyway? A feeling? An emotion? A mood?

What about "discipline"? Is it thoughts or actions, or is that a feeling too? Don't give me your bumper sticker answer either, the one that immediately comes to mind. Give it some thinking. Define it. We all use these kinds of words without really questioning them.

Here's what I've found. When it comes time to make real change in your life, explaining yourself with that kind of shallow thinking makes not one blind bit of difference. I hear it trundled out by new clients all the time—"I just need a bit of self-discipline" or "I don't have any willpower." It's all voodoo! You wouldn't know willpower if it ran over you with a moped! If you are focusing on that kind of answer, you are doing the equivalent of implying that your car runs on stinky bathwater that costs you about four bucks a gallon and that you get your money from the kind lady at the bank, who sits in the back room making twenty-dollar bills out of recycled Target receipts and unicorn snot. Nonsense.

For example, if you're one of life's great procrastinators (and you might be still pondering whether you are or not), it's not as if somebody says, "Yep, you're a procrastinator, take two doses of willpower a day," and BAM! The whole world opens up to you and off you go, motivated as hell and sucking up life goals like sugar-free bonbons on a Sunday afternoon sofa-fest, is it? The fact that you now understand you will need some sort of self-discipline to overcome your procrastinating tendencies doesn't actually solve anything. In fact, it leaves you just as stuck as you've always been!

"Aha, Mr. Scottish man, but I bought that self-discipline book, and I'm going to read it . . . next week."

Sigh.

That's right, you've now got something else to procrastinate with. And the cycle continues. As I've said, knowing a descriptive term for how you live your life just isn't enough. And if what you know isn't making the difference for you, perhaps what you *think* you know isn't what's really going on after all!

Self-discipline is nothing more than doing what you say you will do, when you least feel like doing it.

In other words, acting in a positive way when you most likely *feel* negative. When I say "acting" I don't mean "pretending"; I mean TAKE THE FREAKING ACTIONS! So, if you're waiting for the energy or positivity or enthusiasm or for your chakra to glow a bold yellow, enjoy the wait. It'll be a long one.

What if you are, in fact, *not* a procrastinator anyway? What if it's something else entirely? (No, I'm not referring to some medical condition either.)

I'll give you a clue. No, I take that back, fuck clues, this isn't *Scooby-Doo*. Here's the deal. There's no such thing as a procrastinator; it doesn't exist. It's a descriptive term. A category. There is only someone who procrastinates from time to time and with certain things. We all poop from time to time too, but you don't refer to yourself as a pooper, do you?

"Hello, everyone, my name's Sharon, and I'm a pooper."

Therefore, it's not a case of "I *am* a procrastinator," something you *are*, but rather "I procrastinate," which is something you *do*. And if it's just something you do, then you should do another thing instead. This isn't some personal condition or affliction or something that you "have." It's not a fucking disease.

Sometimes it's a case of just answering the email instead of watching TV. That's hardly a great mystery of life, is it? There may be "experts" out there who offer sympathy and approval to make you *feel* better, but I want to give you the option of an actual better life. And sometimes that fucking hurts. Most of the great things you have done with your life included some level of discomfort, pain, or pressure. That's just how it is. Whatever you are out to accomplish in this life, you'll have to get more than a little okay with the experience of struggle or, hell, even overwhelm. In many ways, your all-out insistence that real-life change should be comfortable is what's holding you down. Growth—real, seismic growth—hurts. Sometimes a lot.

> *"When we are no longer able to change*
> *a situation, we are challenged to change*
> *ourselves."*
> —*Viktor Frankl*

WRESTLING WITH EELS

When it comes down to it, it's as if you are struggling to make your life go in a certain way while at times it seems magnetically drawn in another direction entirely. But you're trying (or at least you've tried), right? It feels like you're constantly wrestling with the things you want and feeling them slither and wriggle out of your grasp. Every now and again you come back to the fight, whether it's with your body or your credit cards or your love life or your career, you see a glimmer of light, and then the whole thing falls apart. Again. In many ways it's like being trapped in the cycle of being *yourself*. Not the great, awesome, idealistic, free-as-a-bird-with-Instagram-pictures-to-die-for self but rather the familiar, cyclical, WTF, own-worst-enemy, here-we-go-again version. *That* self.

You know exactly what I'm talking about here. Those times when it seems like everything is going *relatively* well and then . . . BOOM, you throw a hand grenade in the whole fucking thing. And you can't stop yourself.

Y'know, those times when it seemed like you were "getting along" with your significant other and then, six, seven, or eighty-eight words later, all hell breaks loose and you're suddenly scrambling to find someone with a pickup truck to help you move your shit outta there! Then you calm down. And they calm down. And you mumble some BS apology at each other and then you order a pizza and it fixes things, and then you both kinda forget, but you don't, so you wait for the next incident. And then that one happens. Then the next one. And so on.

So now you're spending $120 a month on make-up pizza while your ass is ballooning faster than a ten-dollar blow-up bed from Walmart. And you argue about that too.

All just because you couldn't stop yourself from saying THAT THING, the one thing you always say. The thing that fucks everything up even though you KNOW you shouldn't say it. And you say it anyway.

So, you take yourself on, bring back those twin devils of "willpower" and "self-discipline," try a bit harder, eat a bit better, and knock out two fields' worth of kale in a week. Then you pull the shit-pin again, and before you know it that slice of pizza that you PROMISED you wouldn't eat somehow magically intertwines itself in your fingers and slithers unnoticed into your mouth like the sneaky little pepperoni bastard cheese-snake that it is, right? Now the problem is pizza and the battle moves to a new front. Damn, maybe the enemy really *is* gluten, huh?

Maybe for you it's that dream job that you worked so hard to get. Six months in and your feet are already getting itchy. *Again*. Or that time you were so proud of yourself for paying down your credit cards only to blow them wide open with a mini you're-only-young-once-I-work-so-hard-I-deserve-it spending spree . . . *again*! Apparently the "only young once" mantra extends well into your forties these days. And beyond.

If you're in your teens, twenties, or thirties, yep, you have a lifetime of this madness ahead of you too. Stick that in your LOL for a minute or so.

Ponder this: What if the point of your life (not anyone else's, remember? YOURS) is to continually and subconsciously set up "the game" of your life, a relentless cycle of sabotage and recovery?

What if very little of how this life of yours has turned out is actually because you haven't met the right person, haven't found the right career/passion, haven't had the courage/confidence/smarts/breaks, or any other reason to which you have turned to explain yourself? What if your life really is a quite intentional and eerily familiar setup for the same results over and over? A conversational trap that you get yourself into but are unable to see, so you spend your life looking in all the wrong places, seeking some kind of answers, but it's all subconscious and you invariably stay stuck?

> *"When the imagination and willpower are in conflict, are antagonistic, it is always the imagination which wins, without any exception."*
> —Émile Coué

When Coué, a nineteenth-century psychologist, spoke of the imagination, he was referring to our subconscious. By "willpower," he meant our conscious, cognitive thoughts. Where these two conflict, the subconscious wins. Always.

So, if the subconscious always wins, and we are wired to constantly play the same game of sabotage and recovery over and over again, are we just terminally fucked? I know this initially sounds pretty grim, but you need to understand what makes human beings so successful. Survival.

SURVIVAL OF THE OBVIOUS

Contrary to popular belief, it's not the strongest nor the fittest nor the smartest who survive.

Dinosaurs alone showed us how wrong that theory is. Some of them were strong, some were smart, but none of them saw extinction coming!

Who, then, is it that survives?

The predictors. Those who can most accurately predict change can adapt to change and therefore survive. The good news is, you are a prediction and survival machine. It's the single reason why we as a species have stayed around as long as we have. Our ability to see things before they happen allows us to adjust and stay safe. We do that by remembering, by keeping score of what's good, what's bad, what's right, what's wrong, what works, what doesn't work, and all via a massive trench of memories stored in the banks of our subconscious for reference and guidance. You have spent your entire life keeping track, looking for familiar keys to where things are headed, and following a life of the familiar.

Every Monday morning looks the same because you are already predicting how it will go before it even starts. This prediction-ism is absolutely *everywhere*.

That first date who showed up late and didn't dress well enough?

Prediction? "Ugh, clearly they don't care. Imagine a life with THAT! Nope . . . bye-bye."

That's it? They walked in fifteen minutes late wearing sneakers and you're done? Yep!

Your ability to predict gives you a greater shot at survival. In this case, you're out to quickly weed out the ones who are a complete waste of your time or sanity before marriage or a long-term relationship. And your tip-top record in pairing yourself with the perfect mate is testimony to your rapier-like accuracy in this field.

Suuuuuuure it is . . .

You predict your relationships, your finances, the weather, politics, your health, your career, you name it.

You have an opinion about how all of that (and more) is going to go.

It's all automatic, spun out by your subconscious in an instant. Hell, there are even things in life you won't take on because you've already determined they're a waste of time for you. *Predictably.*

By your using that same drive to predict and therefore survive, there goes that book you've always wanted to write (prediction: don't know what I'm doing, therefore sure to fail), that new business you wanted to start (prediction: too risky and I'll lose everything I have), the dream to move to Bali (prediction: now isn't the right time, it won't work unless I get more money), the new career (prediction: one day I might be ready for the responsibility, but it would be too hard right now for someone like me), that perfect relationship (prediction: I won't make the same mistakes again, so not until I meet "the one"). There's no end to the possibilities you've written off with nothing more than a series of auto-response triggers in the confines of your head.

"It's too hard."
"It won't work."
"I can't do it."
"I don't know enough."
"There's no point. It won't make any difference."

In terms of survival, what better way to live a long and relatively safe life than to continually barf up the same kinds of issues and problems and then apply the same tired and useless solutions? Your own personal Matrix of old emotions, old complaints, old experiences. Your "no reality" reality.

> *Every day is a new day, right?*
> *No, every day is the freaking*
> *same day.*

I mean, at least you always know what's coming. You also know that you'll survive it too, even if it sucks! No unknowns, no uncertainty, nothing out of left field, no threat to you, just a single, predictable line of engagement. You apply the same eyes and ears to every situation life throws at you and spin in your own mini tempest of the same old dramas and upsets. Circumstances may change, but what stays the same is you and how you see them, as well as how you deal with them and ultimately how you participate in life. The problem here is that it's often hard to see those automatic predictions we're making every day in an effort to survive. It's hard to uncover the themes and story lines that underlie our life events.

But humans are funny creatures, and we're often not content to live a safe, predictable life. We want excitement! Adventure! Passion! And that's the crossroads where human beings exist. Pulled to predict life and stay safe, yet at the same time thirsty for the new and its tempting allure of a better existence. Wanting and lusting after change while gripped by the anxiety of keeping life safe, certain, and survivable. Minimize the judgment, minimize the failure, crush the pain and the uncertainty and the chaos of real change. Safety eventually wins. Survival is the victor.

That's what we call a life. Wanting new; addicted to the familiar. Even when the familiar is as dull as dishwater. When it comes down to it, you'll willingly trade in what you want for what you know. You're doing it right now in your life!

Often when people are stuck in unhappy relationships or unwanted careers, this is what they are *really* dealing with. It's the trade-off. Underneath it all, it's not about the kids or the family or the money or the risk or the judgment of others. It's all survival. Safety over aliveness. Predictability over joy or love or freedom or the life of your dreams.

What makes it so hard to see is that you never fully witness the trap you are stuck in. You only get to live with the consequences of that trap. Your entire life to this point has been a series of actions subconsciously driven to trap you in the same bubble of life.

Take a minute to allow yourself to take stock here. What has been the underlying experience of this life of yours? When it's all said and done, when you look at the struggle and determination, the victories, the defeats, the sorrow, the drive to be happy and content, the seemingly never-ending hunger for something better—better job, better body, better partner, better family, better house, better society, better clothes, better social life, more passion, more purpose, more followers, more whatever, on and on and on—what are you left with?

Pause here for a moment and honestly answer that question for yourself.

Well?

When I ask my clients this question, they mostly have the same answer. "I'm exhausted." Sometimes it's worse.

Sometimes they say, "It's okay."

Fuck!!

Reminder—this works only if you pause and populate this conversation with your own circumstances, your real-life situations and cycles of self-sabotage, to start to draw some sense from what I am saying and how it applies to your life. Do the work here. Start to see the issues of your life through the lens of what I'm saying—your repetitive and destructive behaviors are supposed to be that way! Your life was set up to repeat them. They're also what keeps you being that familiar you, living with the same constraints, weighed down by the past, always in the same, tired struggle for a better day but occasionally sedated by a glimmer of hope or optimism.

Keep in mind, if you really are after some kind of new life, some new and unprecedented result, that will require risk on your part. That will require you to push through your predictable self-talk, your all-too-familiar emotional freeze-frame, and reach for the unknown.

You can't do new without risk. Period.

04

The Magic
Little Sponge

You've deadened yourself to the crap.

By now, you should be able to see that it's not as if you wake up in the morning and say to yourself, "Okay, this is the day when I find crippling fault in my friendships and end them" or "How can I screw with my finances today?" or "Things are great between me and my partner; how can I wreck my marriage?"

If you *are* saying those things to yourself, this book won't save you. Try yoga.

If you're not consciously screwing with your own success, if you're not waking up in the morning and actively planning to undo what you've been building, all on a whim or some deviant master plan, then how did we get here? I've come to realize it must be subconscious. The temptation, the urge, the compulsion, whatever you might call it, driven to the surface from the cellars of your mind and acted upon.

It's not a lack of something on your part. It's more like the presence of something in the shadows. Something you've never really understood that comes to life at moments. Something that shows up like that weird uninvited neighbor to your Fourth of July party.

Let me stop right here and explain a little something about your subconscious. This isn't some self-help, psycho-neuro faffle-babble.

It's real, it's there, and it's working you like an old sock puppet.

David Eagleman, author, neuroscientist, and adjunct professor at Stanford University's Department of Psychiatry and Behavioral Sciences, says, "The conscious part—the 'me' that flickers to life when you wake up in the morning—is only a tiny bit of the operations." Basically, we are being operated on a level we're not even aware of *most of the time.*

And the thing about our subconscious is that it starts off wide open and malleable, yet, over time, becomes set. Rigid. Predictable. How did this happen? Let's take a look.

IT'S ALL OKAY

You weren't always this way, the way you are now. You weren't always making the BS of your life so "okay" that you've become numb to it. You've deadened yourself to the crap. You just shrug your shoulders as if it's "just the way it is" and stumble ahead.

There was an (admittedly brief) life of sunshine and rainbows before this bullshit.

Ask a first grader what they want to be when they grow up. There's not a one among that bright-eyed bunch of future astronauts and superstars who'll testify to their unquenchable, burning desire to be divorced, broke, and unhappy with a withering thud of low self-esteem or a tendency to trash all that's good in their life . . . yet here we are, folks!

Where did it all go *wrong* for you? How did you end up in this trap of sabotaging your life? As with most people, it probably didn't happen overnight. It was a series of seemingly unconnected events in your life where *you* made some important shifts in your perspective until they all came together and left you with a very distinct experience of being alive. *Your* experience of this life, what it is to be you and live life this way, was constructed by you. Period.

The problem is that you had no real sense of doing such a thing. You were just getting on with life, making your way, solving problems, going for it, but the reality is that you formed and shaped yourself through this process of living.

You got yourself here to this point in your life, and I'm going to show you how you subconsciously did it. How you fucked yourself. And how to dig yourself out.

BACK TO THE BEGINNING

Let's take this back. Way back.

Not so much *when* you were born but rather what you were born *as*.

When you arrived on this earth, you hadn't yet developed a subconscious, let alone a personality. There was no repetitive, fundamental, guiding internal dialogue pushing you this way or that. You had no self-defeating opinion of yourself, no suspicious eye for others or resignation about where your life had been or was headed. There was no self-sabotage.

Surely, you've heard of kids being referred to as "little sponges," right? And you've probably seen how kids seem to soak up language and new experiences like thirsty little sponges. Well, in many ways, that's true— we are sponges.* Think about how a sponge works. It absorbs what it comes into contact with, expanding and expanding until it's full of liquid. Then what happens if it's left out to dry? It hardens, trapping any junk that might be left inside of it.

Now, try on the idea that you were born as one of those pristine magic sponges, going through the early stages of life soaking up this thing, squeezing out that thing. As life went on, you never really noticed that the "juice" was drying up, life was becoming more predictable, a little more parched of the new and exciting, until one day that moist magic little sponge within you had hardened. And trapped within its various holes, nooks, and caverns were the items that

---

* You're not really a sponge. It's an analogy to have something make sense. Get with the program, for the love of God!

could never quite seem to be squeezed out. Stained. Locked in there forever. That's how our subconscious works. In the beginning it's clean and untainted, malleable and not yet defined. But now it's set in place, immutable, with a very specific purpose now secured into its very core. One that you can't yet see.

Think about the behavior of babies. Outside of their immediate concerns, babies and infants just don't have a care in that little world of theirs. When I think of my own kids' early experiences of life, it is amazing to think of how little of a damn they actually gave. I was way more fucked up about their lives than they were. They weren't neurotic or depressed, they didn't procrastinate or overanalyze or, in fact, be troubled by anything: they were too busy living the lives they had been thrown into. And their lives were, for the most part, magical. Just like yours was.

I'll never forget the memory of my oldest son, when he was two, jumping into the pool, climbing back out, jumping in again, climbing back out, over and over and over, his face lit up with joy and excitement and adventure. He could not get enough of that one thing, and it never got old.

Until it did. When he got older.

Now, I'm not telling you to become two years old again. This isn't about drooling on your shirt, picking your nose, or stomping your feet when somebody makes you do something you don't want to do either. I know you still do some of that stuff, but that's another thing entirely. There's nothing cool about picking your nose.

What I am talking about is how, back in your early life, everything was new, everything was exciting and pristine. And man, you were curious about all of it. From the smallest thing to the most grandiose, you were all over it. That magic sponge was soaking it all up, filling each crevice, having no idea of the ever-increasing threat of drought. Until the day when everything was set and dried and a life of sabotage unfolded, with a firm commitment to keeping you in a constant struggle.

OF LIMITED BUT VAST POTENTIAL

While you weren't quite born a *completely* vacant little sponge, since you were born *with* certain inherited genetic possibilities and thrown *into* very distinct circumstances (which we'll get into more in the next chapters), there was clearly a massive range of untapped, unwritten ways in which you could have turned out. You were certainly born as a something with a wide-open field of possibilities for who you *could* be. A something with a wide and vast potential.

"Every man is born as many men and dies as a single one."
—Martin Heidegger

Isn't that just a GREAT quote? You were born into a vast spectrum of potential that you've slowly turned into a single item. As you age, your view becomes more and more restricted; you become a narrow, constrained, polarized version of what you started out with. In short, you are addicted to the version of yourself you have become, and your entire existence is about perpetuating that myth.

I mean, think about it. Of all the twists and turns your life has taken, from all those possibilities for yourself, you somehow turned out *this* way.

You're now a very specific, very definitive you with clear-cut characteristics, hang-ups, and familiar emotional states and behaviors.

Also, if you're like most people, you're now spending quite a chunk of your adult life working on improving that "you." Making it fitter, smarter, more confident, less worrisome, more successful, less anxious, more likeable, less insecure, more powerful, less uncertain, more attractive, and on and on and on. You're now a definable, set thing that you have to make better, improve upon, and eventually win over. But why?

CLICKBAIT

In your earliest years, your life was all about what was going on *around* you. It wasn't about *you*. You were gripped by a compelling curiosity about the world you'd been dropped into.

It was all about the discovery of your environment. Your entire life was lived in moments, and you were "there" for all of them.

Oh boy, has that changed.

These days? These days your life is *completely* about you, how *you're* doing, how *you're* not doing, how others are affecting *you* and have affected *you*. It's about fixing *you*, improving *you*, altering *you*, changing *you*. A life of trying to get to that day in the future when it will all turn out in that perfect happy ending you've always imagined.

That "someday" when you eventually "find yourself" through the indigo haze of ayahuasca on the slopes of the Inca Trail or when you get handed that spot on *Shark Tank* or the big promotion you're after or become the next Silicon Valley gazillionaire or Tiffany Haddish or Tom Brady or just a bit more like your idol or older sister or best friend or whatever your thing is, big or small, doable or near impossible.

That day in the future when you're like a fucking ninja and you finally get everything you wanted. And the birds are singing. Yeah, the birds would be there too.

And that's what keeps you stuck. You're trapped in the struggle to be free, yet your thrashing and squirming only keeps you contained right where you are.

There's an irresistible link between happiness and where your attention is pointed. Same goes for unhappiness, of course. When your attention is primarily on what's out of reach, there'll always be something you never quite have. And so, you struggle to have it . . . and on it goes.

If you spend your life wanting to be happy, by its very nature you're constantly starting from a place of unhappy.

You, like all human beings, live each moment of your precious life in the pursuit of something that is, of course, out there in the future, regardless of whether the thing you are after is five minutes or five years ahead of you.

Except the peace or joy or satisfaction you're after isn't "out there" at all.

It's an illusion. It's clickbait for your brain.

That's right, clickbait. You are hypnotically following that ever-so-tempting juicy morsel of hope or stability or success or accomplishment, only to get there and realize that ain't it. I know, not you, you're different. It's other people who do that, and the thing you're after *will* solve your BS—except no, it's you too. That thing you're currently pursuing in your life? The job, the car, the house, the location, the business . . . that's what I'm talking about. You'll get duped. Then you'll do it again and get duped again. And then again. And again. And again. And then you'll die, and that will be that.

For what it's worth, that day in the future will never come. Why? Because even when you do accomplish great things, when you do get *there*, you very quickly realize it's still the same *you*.

YOU haven't really changed. And that's the problem. Different life, same you, and ultimately that's what you're trying to change!

You're not a better you, a more confident you, a more whatever you. It's just the same you with a new accomplishment in the bag, which soon plummets into the black hole of your past accomplishments. It didn't work—that is, it didn't take care of what you thought it would take care of, it didn't bring you the happiness you were looking for—so off you go again. Clickbaiting the hell out of your life.

You might be sitting there right now saying, "Aha, no, Gary, I USED to do that, but not anymore. I've done the work on myself, I've had that realization, and I'm definitely different now." Eh . . . no. You've now set your life up like a fragile game of chess where you've so far been able to avoid, minimize, or suppress what I'm pointing to here.

That's not a life, that's a strategy, and you haven't addressed the impact it has had on your full self-expression and the diminishing of your aliveness and potential. The dulling of your edge.

Settling.

You're as much a diminished version of what you started with as everyone else. Smarty-pants.

CLICK

While neuroscientists can detect the very beginnings of consciousness in the brains of babies as young as five months old, it's not until around two years that we each begin to develop the fully blown concept of a "me," that self-awareness and self-consciousness which tell us that we're an individual, that we're separate from the people and things around us.

Click. Let the games begin. From that moment, your life—what it's about and your special brand of sabotage—starts to get put together.

You start to understand things like embarrassment and possessions and what it is to be wanted and loved and known. You're now confronting the idea that it's "you" in the mirror and that image is what others see when they look at you. You're forming an early opinion of that chubby little ball of innocence.

Many of you still can't deal with that experience to this day. You are uncomfortable staring at yourself, not okay with who you are, and addicted to changing yourself in one way or another.

You're more about self-fix than self-improve.

Thus, you become self-conscious—i.e., conscious of a self—and that self-consciousness carries right on into adolescence and adulthood and all the way to the grave.

Long after the innocence of childhood wonder has dissipated into memories, you make the extraordinary ordinary. Maybe not right away, but certainly over time. Think about the first time you got a cell phone. How about a new car? Your dream home? Remember when that was the most exciting of things? Now? Meh. You're off on search of the next fix. Click.

It's not just material possessions. It also applies to love, relationships, friendships, goals, dreams, and everything else in your life that once upon a time you might have appreciated or treasured. It all gets minimized, made ordinary, and shoved down in the pursuit of something else.

Now pause. Instead of looking ahead, stop right here in this moment to take stock of your life. Think about the dreams or accomplishments or goals that, as soon as you achieved them, withered, added to the shelf in your memory alongside that third-grade reading certificate, first date, college acceptance letter, new job. What was the thing you used to think that, if you just had it in your life, it would make all the difference for you, only to be accomplished and then cast aside in favor of your latest shiny thing?

FLOW

> *"It is understandable that people tend to be so nostalgic about their early years . . . many feel that the wholehearted serenity of childhood, the undivided participation in the here and now, becomes increasingly difficult to recapture as the years go by."*
> —*Mihaly Csikszentmihalyi*

Mihaly Csikszentmihalyi, the guy who coined the now-famous term "flow," tells us that the more complex we become as human beings, at both societal and individual levels, the more we experience psychic entropy—which is a fancy way of saying that the more complex life becomes, the more miserable we're likely to become. Nothing, and I mean NOTHING, can fill the void.

Like everyone, you have fallen into the trap of trying to fill the void by constantly trying to fix what you think is wrong or not good enough about yourself or your life.

To kids, nothing else exists but the moment they're in. It's the ultimate state of Zen, if you think about it. There's no anxiety about the future, no preoccupation with the past. Only now and dealing with the item that presents itself right now.

That's right, you were a fucking Zen baby and you blew it! As adults, we struggle to get to that level of "flow," that same level of unrestrained bliss and presence that marked the simpler times in our lives, so we turn *that* into something to pursue like everything else! These days, you might meditate, pray, do yoga poses, skydive, head off into the wilderness, play sports, read, basically anything you can to get away from the humdrum of the life you have built, to try to squeeze yourself into that most precious glimmer of a present moment, to release yourself from that ticktock drive to get ahead. Driven to try to get your Zen on!

Perspective check: you currently exist on a planet inhabited by millions of species of animals, draped in oceans and mountains with gushing volcanoes and waterfalls and creeping deserts; spinning in an endless universe, with stars and suns and solar systems that stretch wildly beyond anything your limited little imagination can muster—and yet you're fucked up because your job sucks or you are carrying more weight than you want or your nose is bigger than your friend's or your phone is three models older than everyone else's.

That's what this life of yours has come to. A competition. The pursuit of love or admiration or things. You've wrapped up this miracle—your life—in a mundane web of petty, shallow expressions of what it is to be alive. Then you wonder why you're not happy or satisfied or fulfilled! I mean, it's right in front of your face!

I'm not even asking you to be grateful. (Boy, that gratitude thing has been DONE. TO. DEATH.) I'm asking you to check in. To wake up to something a little grander than your belly button and your myriad of trifling concerns.

To begin to take stock of what you have turned this life of yours into.

As you sit here reading these words, this is your opportunity. This is your shot. You, like most human beings, have allowed your life to drift, to meander from one drama to the next without any substantial intervention from you. That's not a put-down but rather something for you to finally come to terms with. Whatever you have done or not done, it just hasn't been the kind of substantive force of nature required to elicit real-life change.

If you truly want to end this, you have to get committed, to give yourself fully to the notion that you are, once and for all, done with the life you have had to this point. It's time to interrupt that drift. Put an end to it.

We're about to paint a picture, some of which you will recognize, some of which might at first seem confusing or maybe even a little surreal, but it will leave you in no doubt that the magic little sponge that you are has hardened. You need to begin understanding what it is that has become trapped in those once eager pores and how you managed to become so hoodwinked by your own game in life.

Remember, we are first building a framework, one you can lay over the confusion of your life and finally make some sense of it for yourself. It's probably not a good idea at this point to start telling everyone you've finally worked it all out and that you're a sponge and all you need to do is figure out what is stuck in the various tunnels and pathways and then you're good to go.

I dunno about *your* friends, but for a lot of people, that kind of outburst might not go down too well. What happens in sponge club stays in sponge club, right?

05

A Throne of Throwns

Ultimately, who is to blame solves nothing. All it does is explain and keep you stuck.

So, you were born a willing and eager magic little sponge free of preconceptions and ready to soak up the exciting adventures of whatever life has to offer. How do we get from there, from that thirsty and enthusiastic stage, to sabotaging ourselves over and over and over?

We are going to start uncovering what got sucked up into those thirsty nooks and crannies of your subconscious. There are two pieces that set the stage for how we come to live a life of sabotage, how that magic sponge becomes heavy and weighted by significance. We'll talk about the first piece in this chapter. And it starts by looking at what you had NO say in.

"HAD NO SAY IN!? Doesn't that make me a victim?"

Well, yes . . . and no.

Look, I know there is stuff in your life that you were either blind to, coerced into, or forced into or any number of ways in which you don't feel as if you had much of a choice in the matter. Fine. You're still on the hook for the quality and success of your life in the aftermath of that stuff. Period.

It might not have been your doing, but it's on you from this moment forward.

What I'm referring to is based on something Martin Heidegger called "thrown-ness." These are the things in your life that you didn't choose, didn't pick, but were *thrown into*. Basically, they existed before you did, and you had to adopt them and adapt to them pretty damn quickly.

Let me explain.

I was born Scottish (we did this already, remember?). I didn't choose that. You might have been born American, Canadian, French, Chinese, or Yemeni. No one gets to choose where or when they will be born. Nor on that fateful day had we chosen our parents or our race or our gender. There is a litany of things you had zero say in but your life is modeled around.

All of that is part of your particular thrown-ness.

Your genetics—how tall you are, what color your hair is, how far apart your eyes are—that's *part* of your thrown-ness. The era you were born into, whether you're a child of the forties or the nineties (or, God forbid, the zeros!), the financial and social status of your family when you were born, the culture, the customs, the language, all of it. Even the very notion of being a human being you had no say in. The fact that there are a sun, a moon, and stars, that there are such things as trees and a society and laws and cars and science and school and that life revolves around seasons—you were thrown into all of it, had it rammed up your nose the minute you were born, and ever since then you have had to wrestle with it to make sense of this madness!

It's all part of your thrown-ness!

That magic little sponge of innocence arrived with a slap and a scream and was thrown into the tide of humanity and the hypnotic trance of "making it."

You had no say in any of this, yet it doesn't matter if you think it's fair. It doesn't matter if you like it, loathe it, resent it, or appreciate it. You're here, and you'll have to deal with it like everyone else before you and everyone after you. This is where the road to peace of mind begins. Acceptance. Acceptance doesn't mean you agree or give up; it means you accept something for what it is and what it's not. Period. You actually can accept what you were thrown into and live a life free from its grasp.

Acceptance is the gateway to real change. It's also something you need to give some real thinking to. You need to deal with yourself and what you haven't really accepted and what you've burdened yourself with by not accepting things as they actually *are*.

> *"Freedom is what we do with what is done to us."*
> —Jean-Paul Sartre

Either way, you're going to embrace all of it (every single, last drop) or you're going to be a victim to it. There's no in-between. Either you'll own it or it will own you. Not all victims look like helpless souls sitting by the wayside of life and pleading for help. Many of them are successful and driven and would balk at the idea of even being called a victim.

Let me break this "thrown-ness" down a bit more. If you're physically bigger (or shorter or wider), you might have found yourself steered to participate in certain activities at school—say, basketball or arm wrestling (okay, maybe not arm wrestling)—and encouraged to like them. If your brain is wired so that you are great at recollecting lots of data, you were most likely someone who was thrown to participate more academically.

Environmentally, maybe you're the kid who got picked last in a sports-centric culture or struggled painfully at math in an academia-centric one. If you grew up in sunny California (the lucky location you were *thrown* into), you might've spent your childhood surfing or skateboarding with certain biases and dos and don'ts, while the kid who grew up in perpetually gray and cloudy Glasgow was inside watching TV or playing football (yes, it's football; it's a ball and you use your feet, for the love of God) in the pouring rain, with an entirely other set of dos and don'ts about life, people, and what's possible.

How in the hell was any of that fair? You didn't choose to be unathletic, or bad at math, or stuck under a giant angry cloud in Glasgow, and you certainly didn't select "bullied" as one of your life choices either as a kid, did you? No, you didn't, but you were thrown in there anyway. No matter where you grew and expanded, each environment was slowly shaping and molding you, and while you could see and explain some of that influence, there were other huge swathes of conditioning you were completely oblivious to. Again, no say in that either. That magic little sponge had a lot of "juice" to choose from. And boy, did it choose.

TREES? WHAT TREES?

There's another thing you were "thrown" into. Conversations.

When I say "conversations," it's not just the general ones of society but also the ones specific to your family and your early environment, the ones handed down from generation to generation about every aspect of life you could care to imagine. A giant, meandering forest of opinions reaching back God knows how long into the past, and you're so deep in it you can't even see it. What were people talking about before and immediately after you were born?

What were the critical conversations going on around you as you grew up?

If, for instance, your parents didn't have a lot of money (and most likely neither did *their* parents), you were born into *their* views and experiences of finances as a scarcity mind-set.

On the one hand, that might have taught you the value of a dollar and to be thankful for what you have. There are plenty of people who break out of that conversational trap and produce great wealth, but it's far more likely you're struggling financially within the same kind of framework your parents were in. Their struggle became part of your conversation.

You might be doing *better*, but you're currently embedded within a group of unspoken financial rules and limits that you had no say in putting together. You *have* agreed to them, though. No one made you do that.

What if you have now become conditioned by your own agreement, to a "glass ceiling," a limit of what you can and cannot do with money? *What if* your adult life is spent trying to reach for that ceiling, not only financially but in every area of your life? What if none of that "trying" was designed to actually get you there?

Self-sabotage is often what shows up when someone starts to hover near financial breakthroughs, when they're getting close to the point of realizing their dream. At this point they realize they'll have to figure out a new, unrecognizable life. Somehow, by seemingly (to them) bad luck or coincidence, they stumble at the last minute and begin to undermine their progress and make the kinds of choices that undo all they were striving for. They return to living within that inherited range of what's possible. The range of the certain.

I've had clients who have built fortunes many times over. A lifetime of trying to get there, fleetingly getting there, and then crashing, over and over. You've had your own version of this in your life too.

Human beings are much more engrossed with the task of getting to the goal than actually achieving it or, God forbid, facing the horror of having to permanently deal with life AFTER they've done the something they'd always wanted to do.

As counterintuitive as it sounds, as a group we are seemingly drawn much more to the struggle than to the prize. That's why, after you succeed, back into the struggle you go. At least that also might start to explain why some people, after accomplishing great things, the fulfillment of long-held dreams and fantasies, follow a path of self-destruction in one way or another to return themselves to their own personal struggle. The history of Hollywood scandal bulges with such tales.

An old coach of mine once asked me, "How good can you stand it?" I couldn't answer him; I had never really considered the idea that there was a "good" beyond the one I was aiming for.

So, how good can you stand it? You might well shock yourself with the answer to that one. If you can tell yourself the truth, that is. The life you currently have would be a clue.

THE SINKING OF THE USS *CONVERSATION*

Those conversations you were thrown into covered every subject of life and, unbeknownst to you, became an important part of what ultimately set the tone for your life of self-sabotage.

Relationships, love, friendships, success, what's good, what's bad, politics, sex, race, faith, you name it, and all fully in existence before you even got here. Some of it was healthy, some of it unhealthy. Some of it was appropriate, some of it wildly inappropriate. Whether your family talked about these subjects openly and in detail or hardly ever or in very vague terms, they all played their part in shaping who you are to one degree or another. As you're probably now realizing, that kind of experience has had a huge impact on you. The impact continues and is still happening every minute of every day and in every area of your life.

You're not unique in this regard. It's the same for every human being on the face of the planet and the ones yet to come.

The adults (and some of the children) from your childhood inadvertently rained wisdom down on your young ears, a wisdom that *you* turned either for or against yourself. But where is all that stuff you heard located? I mean, most of your childhood is all just a blurry mess of thoughts, dreams, and smells that occasionally spring to life when you pass the old neighborhood donut shop or hear your dad's voice when he shouts at the TV. So where did it go?

It sank. It was gulped beneath the waves of your conscious thinking and was swallowed up by the unimaginable depths of the Mariana Trench of your subconscious. And there it all sits. To this day.

I mean, right now it just seems that you're living your life—acting on what's in front of your face, getting things done, watching TV, fiddling around on the internet, meeting people, paying bills (or not), driving your car, going on vacations, making friends, playing sports, reading, writing, daydreaming, getting high, getting drunk, getting off, getting mad—and that none of this old stuff is impacting you at all.

There's plenty of information out there about the degree to which your everyday life is lived at a less than conscious level. Most of it points to the idea of your everyday actions being driven by some unnoticed and subconscious urge or drive for anywhere between 95 percent and 99 percent of the time.

In a paper published in the journal *Behavioral and Brain Sciences*,* a group of researchers, led by associate professor of psychology Ezequiel Morsella of San Francisco State University, took on the question of exactly what consciousness actually is—and came up with a decidedly gloomy view: It's pretty much nothing. You barely control your conscious thoughts at all; it's the unconscious that's really in charge.

Carl Jung, considered by many to be one of the fathers of modern psychiatry and psychology (I prefer to see him as a philosopher and visionary, but hey

---

* Ezequiel Morsella et al., "Honing In on Consciousness in the Nervous System: An Action-Based Synthesis," *Behavioral and Brain Sciences* 39 (2016): e168, doi:10.1017/S0140525X15000643, https://www.cambridge .org/core/journals/behavioral-and-brain-sciences/article/homing-in-on -consciousness-in-the-nervous-system-an-actionbased-synthesis/2483CA 8F40A087A0A7AAABD40E0D89B2.

ho), would have referred to your subconscious as the *unconscious*. It sounds a bit different when you say you're unconscious for most of your life, huh?

Like you're checked out.

In other words, you're running around on autopilot almost all of your day, even with those "mindfulness" practices you've been taking on! It seems like you are in charge, you feel like you're a conscious being, but the reality is, you're not. You're in a haze of automatic thoughts and behaviors masquerading as awareness. That's why when you make a bold commitment to change, you somehow end up right back in that same old routine before you know it.

Every moment of every day, you are being driven to act by your own subconscious thoughts. Caught up in a relentless wave of your innermost self.

THE INVISIBLE YOU

As discussed in chapter 3, we are subconsciously hardwired for safety—seen in the way we automatically do the same predictable things in the same predictable ways over and over and over—while regularly and consciously yearning for something new, something different.

The problem is, the moment you take on something new, those embedded, predictable patterns and behaviors kick in. They sanitize your passion for something new, sober you up with a healthy dose of doubt or dissatisfaction, and draw you to act on the old familiar, safe, and mundane (and sometimes destructive) behaviors that had you stuck in the first place!

The power of the already existing "you" that you've become is too magnetic, too all-consuming, and too powerful. We are conscious beings addicted to the patterns and cycles of our subconscious and automatic reactions to life.

> *"Until you make the unconscious conscious, it will direct your life and you will call it fate."*
> —C. G. Jung

And while you may have a sliver of control over what you consciously think about, you don't actively think about and choose what's in your subconscious. It's a gloomy, shifting mass of everything you've experienced in your life.

You have subconscious influences from your first crush, how often your parents hugged you (or didn't), your goldfish Pete and the image of his little fishy body being flushed down the toilet, the dentist visits, broken bones, your friendships, "experiments" with your body, your failures, shame, successes, and pretty much everything you can imagine. All of it's there in the recesses of your mind, whether it's a tiny blip or a major milestone. Yep, it's all sitting there, deep in the ocean of your most distant thoughts, percolating and pushing you this way and that, all too familiar and ultimately limiting.

You can explain your life, but how much of a say do you *really* have in it as you drift along?

For example, you might know *why* you get angry. You might even have gone to the anger management classes, learned the techniques, and read the books. Like most people, you are probably left with some strategies for avoiding or channeling that anger rather than finally getting to the heart of what it's really all about. That trigger still dominates.

How about my "perfectionists"? You weren't born being perfect, worrying about getting every little detail in your life just right, but you sure as hell have turned out that way. What are you doing about that? How much longer are you going to meander along in the unease and worry of *that* trap? That insatiable appetite for perfection gets hooked, triggered, and irritated by inconsequential and unnecessary BS that at the time seems totally necessary and completely consequential. The unrest and edginess of the desire to have things perfect is followed by the hopelessness of realizing that they never really are.

Then there are the perennially independent people. How are you doing out there all on your own? Maybe you've become too driven or self-centered or think you are some kind of one-man/woman show who can't ask for or even need help. That subconscious strategy of having people think you have your shit together is starting to bite now, huh? That's the problem with being independent: it gets fucking lonely, even when you're surrounded by people.

The reality is, whether you find yourself in these examples or not, you have no idea what specifically constitutes your subconscious makeup or how powerful it really has been in shaping you. You do, however, deal with its impact every single moment of every single day. It's called your life.

The vast majority of what's in your subconscious is ignored, peppered with selective incidents, conversations, and selections of what your cognitive self sees as relative in any moment of time. Jung saw the subconscious as the key to unlocking our potential.

He viewed it as both our biggest weakness and our greatest strength.

"IT'S NOT ME, IT'S THEM!"

Let's deal with the elephant in the book. Many people go the simplest, easiest route when trying to understand why their life took the turns it did. This is also a route we have to destroy now and forever. What's the easy route? Blaming your parents for your life; they're the softest target of all. It's also the most crushing, fracturing, and damaging of pathways to take, not only to them but, more significantly, to you.

Having the parents you had was a big part of what you were thrown into. You had no say in that. However, pointing the finger at them for how you and your life turned out, for your self-sabotage and struggle to get what you want, will never give you the genuine peace of mind and all-is-well-with-the-universe kind of life you are after. Sure, you might use it as fuel for your determination for a while, but you'll always be left with that gnawing, irritating little knot in your being. The back door of excuse will remain, and as long as that's there, you'll use it. It's a boring and humdrum route. The highway to resentment and lack of fulfillment.

Even people who never met or barely knew their parents, or whose parents have passed away, often continue to play that game long into their adult lives. It's obvious. And ordinary. I mean, they gave you life, they made all their mistakes with you, treated you this way or that, spoke to you in the ways that they did, screwed you up. Easy target, right?

Eh . . . not quite. You'll end up stuck in that equation. Some of you are already preparing to unleash the dogs of war right now as I suggest this topic. Wind it in. Read on. You need this more than most.

If you're reading this as meaning I'm getting ready to take sides, you're absolutely right: I AM.

I'm taking YOUR side here! But that doesn't mean you and I are going to agree. I have a feeling we might well disagree. Fine. You're the one who's self-sabotaging here, though, not me (at least not right this minute). It's time for a change. Your change. You with me here? Read these words with that kind of commitment in mind. A commitment to change.

Before you start throwing anyone under the bus, remember that everyone in your life was thrown into the fire, just as you were, and has lived inside the trap of *their* inherited BS, just as you have done. I know, I know, when you were growing up, your parents were supposed to have all the answers, all the wisdom, supposed to have been perfect human beings like your friend's parents or the ones you saw on TV, right?

Still think your parents should have known better? Yeah, maybe they should have. But also, right now, so should you, and how has that worked out?

We're all human beings, trying to make it, often failing, sometimes disastrously so.

Perhaps your relationship with your parents is "okay."
It's often not a good sign when you describe any part
of your life as "okay," let alone some of your most
important relationships.

Maybe you have already dealt with this and cut your
parents out of your life, so you're feeling pretty good
about yourself right now . . . nope, that ain't it, either.

Listen to me carefully. The single most important thing
you can do for your life is to release *anyone* (including
yourself!) from blame for how your life has turned out.
This includes parents, friends, neighbors, everyone.
If that irritates you or enrages you, if you find yourself
turning to your go-to argument or all-too-familiar
upset, take some stock here. You are arguing to keep
the life you have. You're making a case for sabotaging
yourself!

Notice how you are completely *run* by that emotional
trigger. What are you doing to *yourself*? What are
you filling your life with? Suppressed anger? Quiet
resentment? Clinging to the idea that you're broken or
dead inside? Really? Is this worth it? I mean . . . come
ON!!!

It's time to stop blaming your parents, or anyone else
for that matter, for where you've now landed in life.
That explanation has run its course. It's tired and worn
and out of juice. Even if you were thrown into the
worst circumstances, it's your choice now to turn your

life around, make it better, learn and grow and break free of where you came from. You have choice from this moment on.

I GOT YOU, WHETHER YOU LIKE IT OR NOT

Listen, I know there are plenty of people who will sympathize with you, who will look at what I'm saying here as if I'm some kind of bully, or I don't know what I'm talking about or what people go through, or I have zero compassion for others. Nothing could be further from the truth.

Here's the deal—YOUR REAL LIFE is lived in moments, and whether you like it or not, you're *always* in this moment.

> *I find it funny when people say "Be in the moment," as if there's some kind of freaking alternative. You're always here. You're just not always here for what's here.*

The question is, what are you *doing* with this moment, right fucking now—what are you using it for? Are you spending these precious moments of your life bathed in resentment about the life you were thrown into, the genetic facts you can't change, or the web of conversations that have kept you trapped under a glass ceiling? Or are you finally willing to release yourself and everyone in your life from the blame?

Ultimately, figuring out who is to blame solves nothing. All it does is explain and keep you stuck.

That's your choice here. It really is black and white.

Choose. What are you going to fight for? The past or the future? Your self-sabotaging BS or a long-awaited freedom?

In this very moment, you're doing either what you usually do or something else entirely. That's always the case until you die. Moment by moment.

Perhaps it's time for you to get interested in that something else. You cannot free yourself with conditions. Either it's free or it's not.

You have to be willing to own your life for how it is, no blame, no anger, no resentment. It went the way it did, you turned out the way you did, and now it's game on and into the future we go.

Don't know how to do that? Aha! I have the very thing just for you!

Take a moment here and look back at your life. In particular, look at your background and upbringing. Now, what are all the ways you have used that thrownness to justify yourself?

What do you justify? Your bad temper? The three dollars in your bank account? Your past relationships? That you didn't go to college or failed there? Your body shape? Your sense of self-worth? The quality of your friendships (or lack thereof)?

Dig into this a little. Take your time to uncover all of the ways in which you look to the stuff you had no say in to explain the life you now have.

You were thrown in; you had no choice in it. Now, own it!

Think of this like outsourcing. Your life has been about explaining and justifying and excusing yourself, in effect giving away your power to outside influences. But now, it's about bringing all that stuff back in-house, about getting your life together and recognizing yourself as the one and only true source of change.

It's you, and it always has been. Bring it home, baby!

Let's crack on.

06

Establishing the Truth

Your "truth" and "the truth" are not the same, even though you have designed your life around the idea that they are.

We have the first two foundational parts down: what you were born *as*—a magic little sponge; and what you were thrown *into*—a certain life with ready-made conditions that you had no control over. That now requires us to uncover the final piece of the equation that completes the groundwork before we start uncovering your unique saboteurs. It's worth reminding you that understanding the background I'm putting together here will allow you to make sense of yourself in a very real way.

I call this next piece your "established truth."

Basically, your formative years were all about establishing the truth. Your truth. Your subconscious map of reality coming together. Your truth about you, the world, the people around you, everything.

I should say here, very clearly, your "truth" and "*the* truth" are not the same, even though you have designed your life around the idea that they are. You have no idea what *the* truth is, although you would swear that you do.

Your gravitational draw for self-sabotage is, as we've already discussed, designed to repeat and repeat and repeat. But it's also built on an illusion, the illusion of how you have seen your life to this point. As we discussed, that past of yours started with what you were thrown into, but that really was just a beginning.

Whether you'd say you have had a crappy life, an uneventful one, or a great one, your future is perpetually hampered by however you describe the past, though not in the way you might think it does.

Our past is the template upon which our entire future is based; therefore, it's little wonder we live such lives of limitation and frustration.

Most people, if you ask them, will explain how their life has turned out by looking to a series of selective milestones. Some will take three minutes to tell you and others will take a mind-numbing three weeks, with more twists and turns than a bowl of ramen noodles and of much less interest than our squiggly friends of economical delight.

How would you describe how life has gone for you thus far? What are the milestones you'd point to? Whatever falls out of your mouth here is your established truth.

Basically, you have a tale to tell like everyone else, a ready explanation of yourself, your life, and why you now do what you do. As you stumble your way through your daily life (and yes, it's a stumble), you refer back to this "truth," occasionally recollecting the tired and well-rehearsed lines to justify and explain yourself—and, every once in a while, to try to understand yourself.

We've come up with standard ways to justify and explain how we are as adults. We use the same *kinds* of explanations, and we accept those explanations from others so that they'll accept them from us.

It's the kind of stuff you talk to your close friends about after your second or third drink when the conversation innocently slides away from the topic of your favorite Netflix show and into why you're struggling these days. You connect the chaos or discomforts of your life today with some hurt, pain, or incident from your past.

You blissfully explain your life away in the same way your parents would explain theirs and your grandparents would explain theirs. This method of explanation gets handed down from generation to generation in the everyday meanderings of conversation. The details differ, but the bullshit continues.

Any random stranger could walk up to you, ask you to tell them a little about yourself, press the INFO button, and off you'll go.

You'll start with what you do for a living, where you work or live, and within the space of a few nudges of conversation out it comes:

"I'm originally from Buffalo, and . . ." or "I'm the youngest of three, so . . ."

Or "I was born in the eighties, which is why . . ." or "My father was a Marine, and . . ."

Or "My mom was a teacher, so . . ."

Now, most of that stuff is just plain old-fashioned thrown-ness you're talking about, stuff you had no say in. You had no say in your dad being a Marine, right? But you and I both know it doesn't end there, does it?

Oh, hell no. Because next comes the juicy stuff!

Stuff like "Dad was a Marine and was too strict with me as a kid. I don't think he really cared about me. He seemed more interested in his career than in how I was doing. It was like I could never do anything right in his eyes. I became a bit of a loner in my teens and never really broke out of that."

You can see where people might start shaping their lives around such statements. Changing themselves or their circumstances to avoid or suppress certain things. Building a life. Establishing a truth.

UNTRUTHING THE TRUTH

Okay, let's do a little exercise.

Imagine you're holding a cup of hot, black coffee. Suddenly, out of nowhere, someone bumps your elbow and the scalding liquid goes everywhere! It splatters across your bare arm, down your leg, all over the floor. The burning pain is intense, the mess irretrievable. Your pants are completely ruined, and you have a job interview in twenty minutes! You need to change clothes *now*!

Except you can't. You're in a Starbucks. You're miles from home, and your interview is a fifteen-minute walk away.

You look at the guy who crashed into you and say, "Seriously, man?"

He shrugs his shoulders and mutters a barely audible apology, quickly walking away. Like he doesn't give a damn.

Your heart is racing, your head a mishmash of thoughts, your body pulsing with anger, then frustration, before subsiding to helplessness and then down to resignation. It took ages to get this interview! You're screwed. You leave and head home.

Okay, now imagine you are someone else who is *watching* this same scene from a corner of the Starbucks. Instead of the participant in it, you're now an observer of it.

You're quietly enjoying your morning tea and muffin when a guy comes in and catches the corner of your eye. He looks agitated, a little nervous. He orders a coffee, reaches for his wallet, takes out his credit card, and then drops it.

"Dammit!" he proclaims in a biting tone. He pays and steps to the side, past several other people between himself and the pick-up counter.

"Timmy!" says the server.

"Eh, it's TOMMY, actually," he retorts. (I'm fully aware that no one is really called Tommy anymore.)

Tommy grabs his cup, briskly turns, obviously not looking where he is headed, and BAM! He smacks right into a young guy who didn't see him coming.

Tommy's coffee explodes everywhere.

"SERIOUSLY, MAN!!!?" exclaims Tommy.

The entire room silences as everyone turns to find the source of the drama.

The young kid, clearly embarrassed and trying to get away from this spectacle, softly apologizes and makes a hasty retreat.

AAAAAAAAAND SCENE!!!

Now, which of these versions is "the truth"?

Well, both of them are. In the first scenario, you personally experienced the man bumping into you, which seemingly caused you to miss a job interview. In the second, where you were observing rather than participating, you saw both parties at fault for different reasons. If you had seen or experienced only the first scenario, you'd think the fault was completely on the other man. That's the tricky thing about truth: we see it only from our own perspective. But what I want you to consider is that this exercise is your entire life in a microcosm. What you have relied upon as the truth is nothing more than your personal experience of incidents and circumstances, except that in your case you have carried these experiences around, as if they were carved in stone, and fabricated a life out of them.

"Oh yeah, Gary, but what about speaking *my* truth, huh?"

That's fine, but what if "speaking your truth" is what keeps you trapped? For what it's worth, I'm fine with anyone speaking their truth, just so long as you realize that's just what it is, how it was for *you*. That doesn't diminish or pooh-pooh your experience; it just allows you to see it in a way that empowers rather than victimizes you.

You are a magic little sponge permeated with a myriad of established truths upon established truths. Is it any wonder many people have trouble getting free from their past? They're looking in all the wrong places, arguing with family and friends, trying to reconcile a past that *they* see as "the truth" with people who obviously had an entirely different experience from theirs.

Then they get furious about that! Your truth is NOT the truth to anyone but you, and if your truth does not light you up, it might be time for you to come up with another one. If this sentence infuriates you, that should give you a sense of how committed you have become to your own version of the past rather than confronting the life you've forged since those times and the future you are currently denying yourself.

Take a look right now and start to deal with what you've done with your life. Look at your relationships with your family, with yourself, the way you relate to love and sex and your potential and partnerships. Your hang-ups, your triggers, your rages, and your disappointments.

All of it based in, organized around, interwoven with . . . what?

Your established truth. Your version.

Let's go back to the example of the kid whose dad was a Marine. Here, it wasn't the fact that she was the daughter of someone in the military that compelled her to turn inward. Lots of people come from that background and have very different outcomes. It was the established truth she connected herself to that did the damage. Her established truth became what she told herself about the way her dad was more interested in himself than her, which led her to a life of being a loner.

Dad did what he did. That's it! What she did with her established truth from there was on her. It doesn't matter how shitty your past was. Many people have had upsetting or devastating experiences in their past that, as adults, they've tried to forget or managed to "overcome" by trying to put a positive spin on them. They fool themselves into the idea that they're "over it" or that it no longer impacts them. They're trying to get over something they took away from their already skewed and biased lens of the world.

I can completely understand that you might have been thrown into a life that included things that were blatantly inappropriate, often unjust, and in some cases even illegal or immoral. I get that. I have all the compassion in the world for you if that's the case. My heart truly bleeds for you and what you experienced, but at the same time my head wants to give you a shake!

Your established truth lives on through you. You perpetuate it. It's all yours now.

Once established, these truths of yours go deeper and reach further out and begin to take over your life, reaching all the way back from the past and crawling into your future like an existential shadow. You're hooked on them. And I mean hooked.

It's as if you're stuck in your own personal *Groundhog Day*, except this isn't funny anymore and Bill Murray isn't coming along anytime soon to help you out with some of that caustic, dry wit and his cheeky midwestern grin.

Who or what have you blamed for your life being the way it has been? Maybe your life was turbulent and upsetting when you were growing up, or perhaps it was boring and uneventful. The thing is, there are plenty of people who grew up in similar situations who haven't turned out anything like you.

Or maybe you came from a comfortable, peaceful home and had the childhood of your dreams! What did you establish as true about that?

Look, lots of people have dirt in their past. Some were made bankrupt, some were assaulted or robbed or cheated, while others were dominated by others and used for a purpose outside their wishes, but that kind of stuff does not define you or who you are. Who you have become is not a function of what happened back then but rather of the "truths" you picked out and held onto.

In our exercise there was a coffee shop, some people, and some spilled coffee.

THAT WAS IT, NOTHING MORE!! But if you were to ask a few people about the incidents and what they saw, you'd hear different perspectives, opinions, judgments, and unabashed drama.

Imagine all of that getting stuck in that magic little sponge! What would that do to a life? Consider the idea that your entire life is nothing more than your personal experience of it. An angle. A way of looking at your life that became much more than just a simple viewpoint. It became an excuse for why you keep falling into the same destructive patterns. But it doesn't have to be.

A CURVEBALL

What you've been pointing to as "truth"—every incident, every scene, every drama, joy, and upset from your childhood all the way through to five minutes ago—is little more than a perspective. It's not *the* truth. It's an angle from which you participated in the life you were thrown into. Everyone has one of those.

Which one is "the" truth?

None of them . . . or *all* of them. But not *one* of them.

You've lived as if your "truth" is objective, like a solid, immovable object that *is* the way it is. But it's not. And that's why we argue—in politics, in relationships, in business, and in our families. Painfully trying to reconcile, to agree on a single truth, when the reality is that there is none.

On one hand, you can never change the past, but on the other, you *can* choose to change how you see and explain it. Which in turn changes how you feel about it. Which then, in every sense of the word, changes the past for you. At the very least how it impacts you.

This news could also be terrible for you. Why? Because you may well have witnessed your family disintegrate or your love life founder or your dreams crash because they were organized around your version of events. And you fought for your version. You became dug in about your version, and you've been right about it ever since.

Your truth, your view, as if it were the only truth, the only view. Screw everyone else and how they experienced things, right?

Explaining your current life could now become a bit more challenging, given this news. Uh-oh!

It's at this point of the inquiry that many people start to panic. They cop out and myopically blame genetics or some intangible mystery of life that they seemingly cannot have or change. The need to excuse and explain is compelling. You'll pivot and start to rationalize that some people are just smarter, more gifted, or superlatively stronger or more intuitive than you, basically ANYTHING to get you off the hook for how this life of yours has been going.

You might start claiming that I'm discrediting or diminishing the severity of your experience and that no one can possibly understand your "journey." Maybe I'll become yet another of those people who never understood you or don't "get" you. Then you can throw this book down in a hissy fit and head back to your BS life.

Just so you know, I'm face-palming the shit out of myself right now.

You? You're victimizing yourself into a truly forgettable life. Like most people, you'd rather explain your life than intervene in it.

Oh well, you're fucked, might as well just go live in a cave in the mountains, huh?

Give me a break. I'm not backing down, and neither should you.

Your past is basically an explanation, something you came up with to explain why you are you. Period. An excuse. This shit has just got to end.

The French Existentialist Jean-Paul Sartre sums it up perfectly here:

> "Like all dreamers, I confuse disenchantment with truth."

Look, at some point, you just *have* to get sick of yourself and your justifications, but do it in such a way that you don't become victim to yet *another* thing. This isn't about despair, or guilt, or shame, or any other negative state; this is about finally taking total and complete ownership of your life. Dry your eyes, sit up in your chair, and finally set the record straight with yourself.

Whatever truth you own doesn't own you.

If you're still struggling with this, start with the idea that at some level you get something out of keeping your established truths the way they've been. Something gets proved and confirmed by your continued squirming and avoiding taking ownership of your life. To separate yourself from the damage *you've* done.

So, you think you're fucked up because you were born in a trailer park and you never saw your drunk dad, or your parents divorced, or you were bullied at school, or someone betrayed your trust or manipulated you as a kid? Maybe you were a standout sports star at school and now just a washed-up has-been. Maybe you didn't flourish at school at all and now *that's* why you don't pursue a life that requires some academic or intellectual application.

Really? Sure, your life might be off track or, hell, even in the gutter right now, but your established truths you use to explain it just don't cut it in the cold light of day anymore. Not after what you've just read here. That truth doesn't own you.

Stop squirming! I can hear you now: "But other people have drive/ambition/purpose, and I don't have that."

So, that's what your life has come down to? A feeling? A momentary surge of your emotional state? You're waiting on a passion suddenly rising? That's why you haven't broken out of this cycle? Listen closely. You're not any different from anyone else! You have all of this untapped potential, a greatness, a contribution to make to this life and to people, yet you spend your days explaining yourself away!

You're going to have to confront the idea that you are in fact *not* defined by your established truths and that they are nothing more than a shiny, easy-to-explain excuse for your life, just like your thrown-ness. They are your heavy, significant, and justified get-out-of-jail-free card.

In short, the jig is up. You do not self-sabotage because of mommy issues or daddy issues or trust issues or confidence issues or anything else. You don't even have issues! We did this before—you're not a category! This isn't about what was done to you or what has happened to you or where you are from or your genetic luck of the draw.

You self-sabotage because of something else entirely . . .

Your sabotage is completely a function of the *three saboteurs*. And it's now time we unmask them.

> *"There's simply no polite way to tell people they've dedicated their lives to an illusion."*
> *—Daniel Dennett*

07

The Three
Saboteurs

You are in a
perpetual state of
fucking yourself
over so that you
can repeatedly
save yourself
from what
fucked you over
in the first place!

If you haven't taken a break until this point, take one now. There has been a lot to take in, and the next part will be all the more impactful if you've had a chance to percolate with everything we've covered.

- You were born as a magic little sponge, open and willing and ready to absorb everything the world was presenting you with.
- That magic little sponge was thrown into a life it had no say in. Whether genetics, family situation, location, or circumstance, there was nothing you could do about it.
- You are stuck with whatever you have held on to, from what you were thrown into AND what you established as true. But your established truth is just a perspective; it does not own you.

All of this combined to give you a dramatic backdrop against which to live your life. A scene that you get to play out every night in front of an audience of one. You.

If you need to, go back and review to make sure you're set and ready for what's next. Specifically, think about what you were thrown into in your life. What are the things you couldn't control? In what ways have you been telling yourself that these things have shaped you? What established truths do you have about things in your past? Where have you gotten stuck?

Think of this chapter as a little bridge. It takes us from the groundwork we've laid, on one side, to what's at the very root of your subconscious, on the other. This is the point in the book where we start to reveal the deepest of conversations in your subconscious that drive you to live life the way you do and to be who you have become.

This is why you can't break out of your patterns of self-sabotage. *This* is why your life is in a cycle of BS that you occasionally break out of, only to return. Everything I have talked about has been to get you here.

You see, there are three pivotal and everlasting items, three fundamental cornerstones of life that came out of that thrown-ness, that arose from that myriad of established truths that became locked in that magic little sponge. Immovable and permanent stains on your subconscious that shape and contort everything you see and everything you hear.

I call these the "three saboteurs."

The three saboteurs are the focal point from which all things must begin and to which all things must return, no matter how far you reach, no matter how great your life could be. You have an internal compulsion to return to them, no matter what damage that might do.

Let me break down what a "saboteur" is.

A saboteur is a subconscious conclusion that you made at a definitive point of your life, the kind of indelible mark that stays with you to this day. It will remain with you until the day you die.

You can shift how you relate to your past, you can free yourself from the weight of your emotional baggage, but you cannot change or erase what you have fundamentally concluded. It just is, and it always will be.

That might sound like bad news. But the discovery of your unique conclusions might well be just the shift you need to get and keep your life on track.

I like to think of my saboteurs as my own little lighthouses in the night. When I encounter them, they're a warning that I'm about to start drifting into my predictable default life. My self-fulfilling prophecy. When I recognize them, I'm able to pivot. When I use the words "awareness" or "self-aware," this is what I'm referring to. An up-close and very personal relationship to your own wiring; a relationship that gives you in-the-moment options instead of just fate.

You are guided by these three simple conclusions, and if you look closely enough you will be able to identify yours by the effect they are having on you and your life.

Your actions are *always* in alignment with your conclusions. You might not immediately see the pebble drop into the pond, but you will see the ripples it leaves behind.

CONFUSING CONCLUSIONS

So, what are these conclusions? How can you start to identify them in your own life?

By the end of the first two decades or so of life, the formative years when your physical and neurological development was at its most defining, you, like all human beings, had arrived at a set of fundamental conclusions about three things:

- Yourself
- Others
- Life

These conclusions are each very different, have unique and distinct ways of showing up in your life, and, when combined, are loaded against your potential. They skew everything. Contort everything.

And ultimately burden you with the life you currently have. The one you're trying to change.

Before you get your knickers in a twist, relax. I'm going to go into each of these three in detail in the next few chapters. In the meantime, consider that every single day of your life you are viewing the world via a small, tightly wound network of your own doing. A constant internal framework that you unconsciously picked up and stored for future guidance. To keep life safe and survivable. The same.

That's the paradox here too. That framework is what compels you to get better and improve (and take risks), but at the same time the framework itself needs constant reassurance of its existence because it's what keeps you safe.

Let me be a little more agricultural about this. You are in a perpetual state of fucking yourself over so that you can repeatedly save yourself from what fucked you over in the first place!

Day after day, week after week, year after year, you see *yourself* in the same way, you see *others* in a very distinct way, and you see *life* in the same way you always see it. Talk about predictable!

Let's dive in. And let's start with the saboteur that might hurt the most: yourself.

08

You

*You've become
so fascinated
by your own
temporary
solutions, so
seduced by
the mirage of
the future, that
you can't see
it's an illusion.*

The first saboteur we're going to dive into is what you've concluded about yourself. I call this your "personal conclusion."

That's right, you've come to a pretty damning, repetitive conclusion about yourself. There's an all-consuming whisper going on in the abyss of your subconscious. It runs in the background of your thoughts, humming along, prodding and poking you, enticing you to work on yourself, but eventually returning you to the whisper. And it's personal.

This is where your pathway to understanding and finally ending your self-sabotaging behavior begins. Until this point, we have been setting the groundwork with some abstract ideas about how we became the people we are today, but now it has to get real for you. This is the first and most primary conclusion you will need to understand to finally get yourself out of this pattern of sabotaging your life.

Here's how your personal conclusion came to be. During your formative years, you inadvertently captured a handful of "treasured" items in that magic little sponge—some you picked up in early childhood, others a little later—about who you are and how you see yourself, your capabilities, and, most significantly, your shortcomings.

Especially those shortcomings, because conclusions are *never* positive.

Let's get something out the way. Don't start by telling me your personal conclusion is "I'm freaking awesome!" It's just not.

You might occasionally say that to yourself with a dimple in your cheek and an eyeball-piercing glint from those ever so well-polished teeth of yours. Hell, at some superfluous level you might even believe it, but the truth of it is, it's the shellac of bullshit people tell themselves to "overcome" what's underneath the surface. It's a scheme to stomach life, to somehow put some My Little Pony glitter on the immovable density of your most ignored, tolerated, and to-be-improved self.

It's a criticism, an internal, repeating criticism of self. The flaw that people are referring to when they roll out the old "I'm not perfect" line to make themselves look good to others.

The reality is, a lot of people don't even realize the conclusion they have come to believe about themselves because they're too busy, too focused, too ensnared in the life they're trying to build that they never take stock of why they are living this way!

You've become so fascinated by your own temporary solutions, so seduced by the mirage of the future, that you can't see it's an illusion. Like the trapped little fish that comes to the surface of the tank every time you dangle your fingers above. Every single time, you get hoodwinked.

Your negative conclusions don't mean you can't experience happiness or joy or optimism. We all experience life in those ways too, but what I'm talking about is that "baseline" self, the one on which everything in your life is modeled.

You don't walk around with these conclusions *constantly* on your mind or at the very top of your to-do list while you're going to the supermarket or getting on a train or spread-eagled on the sofa getting your regular *Game of Thrones* fix.

Rather, your conclusion is the Vaseline smear across your view of your day-to-day life, slightly blurring and obscuring everything you see and occasionally coming into view.

(Unless you're failing at something. Oh, if that's the case, then it's right in your face and choking the life out of you.)

Your personal conclusion is like a never-ending, never-changing internal guide. It keeps you pegged to the life you have, and it always comes back to mind, no matter how good life gets. It's kinda like trying to hold a beach ball underwater. You can do it for a while, but eventually, up it comes.

Of course, the conclusion about yourself is the negative, but you're also out to make yourself and your life better, so . . . along comes a handy positive every now and again to help you handle it, to temporarily leave you with the feeling that you actually ARE okay, that you're on track and that this WILL turn out for you, and sometimes the illusion that it HAS turned out after all! Then it comes back. That's the seesaw of your life right there. That's the range within which you exist, back and forth, up and down. Two steps forward, two steps back. And that's how you are wired to live! Right there! Circumstances change, you remain the same.

In many ways, your circumstances are nothing more than context that your conclusion gets to dance with. Everybody's working on their circumstances. Is it any wonder the conclusion remains?

Your conclusion about yourself always begins with an "I."

It's stuff like this:

"I'm not smart enough."

"I'm a loser."

"I'm different."

"I don't matter."

"I'm incapable."

"I'm not loved."

Or even all the way down the hole to "I'm worthless."

You might identify with one of these or none of these. The question you need to answer is "What have I concluded about *myself*?" This is the fundamental experience of yourself, the inherent design that you continually try to overcome and yet somehow always end up with again. Your particular conclusion.

It's the thing you say to yourself when no one is looking, when there's nothing to prove, no one to impress. Just you and your thoughts.

It's about *you*. No one else, nothing outside of you or some circumstance you're dealing with. You. And *for* you, when all is said and done, it's the *truth of truths* when you are pressed by life and no one can tell you any differently.

For example, if you're burdened by the conclusion "I'm not smart enough," all those years of teachers or your mom or your friends telling you that you *are* smart made no difference. To you, they just didn't get it. Maybe they treated you like there was something wrong with you, or maybe YOU thought there was something wrong with you! No amount of accomplishment, recognition, certification, knowledge, hints, systems, or praise will release you from the grip of your own conclusion. No matter the prize, you're eventually left back where you started. "I'm not smart enough." It's *never* enough or, rather, you're never enough.

Think about that for a moment.

> *Think about that persistent, pressing experience you have of yourself in this life.*

Connect the dots here.

I'll help you out with an example of a very common personal conclusion that some people have: "I'm a loser."

Now imagine your life with *that* permanently in the hazy background of your thoughts. Every time you're pressed, stressed, or fail at something, up it rises.

"I'm a loser, I just knew it, here we go again, what is wrong with me, why can't I get anything right?"

It produces a stream of connected thoughts and emotions, all automatically. The kind of thoughts that bind to that fundamental conclusion. It grows arms and legs, the conversation swells—"I can't do it," "It's too hard," "It's too much." It's not just a thought or a background noise. When it's triggered, when it's loud, you're *in the world* of that thing. It controls you.

Imagine a *lifetime* of that. Imagine the bone-crushing impact of *that* when you get fired or your partner leaves you or someone else gets that promotion or your best friend just announces that they've nailed that dream job testing organic suntan lotions in Tahiti while you toil away trying to sling thirty-bucks-a-month cell phone cards from the back of your crumbling car.

Now you can see why positive thinking or personal affirmations of "I am enough" or "I am successful" seem so fake, so fucking useless and weak, because deep down, at the very heart of you, there's a gnawing pain. You are a loser, and no one can convince you any differently.

And guess what? Not everyone who has that kind of internal conclusion lives in a van down by the river! No!

They're lawyers and doctors and teachers and every kind of "successful" member of society you could imagine. Going about their lives with the conclusion that fundamentally, *they* are something less, something not quite up to par. Every morning they get out of bed, shuffle into the shower, get dressed, shove some coffee down their throat, and plunge into their usual day. When they get to work, it's game on, pretending their conclusion isn't there. Avoiding or manipulating people and situations that remind them of their own conclusion.

They're keeping it hidden from view, guarded, pushed out of mind, out of sight. That's their struggle. The daily battle between their worst self and the limit of what they see as possible, a limit that has been pulled down, shrunk, and diminished over days and weeks and months and years.

> *Is it any wonder we have become so resigned to the lives we have?*

"We are what we pretend to be, so we must be careful about what we pretend to be."
—Kurt Vonnegut Jr.

You lose sight of *when* you started doing this shit and *why* you started doing it, and you get so wrapped up in its drama and significance that you actually believe it to the bones of your being.

Again, it's not as if you are going around in life *constantly* in that dialogue with yourself. It's more that your life is systematically organized around what you have concluded.

These are obviously not the kinds of things you're super eager to tell people about either. It's not as if you saunter into work and share your deepest fear with your boss while chomping into your second all-natural Amazonian walnut energy bar of the day with one hand and mashing out your desperate-cry-for-help email with the other, now, is it?

In fact, you have already fashioned your entire being around keeping your conclusions discreet.

I mean, you have to! What would people really think of you if *they* knew how you saw yourself? Therefore, you live your life in that constant state of overcoming, of pretending and posting pictures on Instagram of the person you want to be, or at least the person you want other people to see you as.

Some of you are in so deep, so lost in the Matrix, that you can't bring yourself to look at what I'm saying. You're already dismissing it without any real introspection or writing it off because you can't seem to work this out for yourself.

This isn't a movie, this is your real life, and in this case you are both the rebels and the Matrix. It's all you.

Try on the idea that your life—how you look, how you speak, where you live, how you live—is all to project a certain image of yourself while at the same time hiding another version of yourself from public view—the one you really believe to be true.

Are you hard at work keeping your shit together to keep your life at a certain level or to get to a new one? For what purpose?

Why is your success so important to you? What are you trying to overcome?

I'd argue it's the way you try to deal with, to somehow handle or wriggle free from, the weight of your personal conclusion, which is constantly burrowing away inside you. The first of the saboteurs.

THE SCROOGE IN ALL OF US

One of my favorite books is *A Christmas Carol* by Charles Dickens. If you've never read the book, you've most likely heard of the central character, Ebenezer Scrooge. The reason why I love this story goes well beyond the obvious. You see, our old friend Scrooge is a case study in everything I've been talking about thus far. In fact, after reading this book, you might well never look at that tale in the same light ever again!

When Scrooge looked back on his life, he began to experience the discomfort of how he had shaped himself, something that he had always blamed on others. He says: "These are the shadows of things that have been. They are what they are, do not blame me!"

He couldn't be with the notion that he had hardened *himself*, that his cynicism was a self-imposed exile after he lost the love of his life. He had concluded that he could never have love or be loved and built his life around that conclusion. He constructed a reality where he found fleeting joy, a slew of temporary fixes, accruing more and more money, but the conclusion he had made ate away at him day after day. No one could get in, not even his loved ones. He dismissed their approaches out of hand. He could not see what was right in front of his face, as it was a massive contradiction to his own subconscious belief, so he plowed on anyway, perpetuating his own conclusions and denying anything that might be a threat to that reality.

Just like you do.

GRAB A SHOVEL, WE'RE GOING IN

So, what have you concluded about yourself?

That's what you need to consider here. And the only way to do it is with a thorough examination of your own experience of being alive. This is where you need to do the thinking.

Right now, get straight with yourself. Take a look behind all the BS, all the hope, all the wants, needs, and plans for the future. Forget the past, forget the reasons, justifications, and excuses—what is the underlying dilemma you face with yourself? This isn't about money or your lifelong obsession with becoming a hand model (specializing in thumbs). Dig deeper. Take a long, hard look at those times in your life when you're most struggling, most tested. What is it that comes up for you? You cannot move from this chapter until this is solid.

Do you avoid parties or social settings and say it's because you don't like them? Or is it really because you are driven by the discomfort and pressure that arises from the conclusion "I don't fit in" or "I'm different" or "I'm not enough"? The fear of being revealed can do that to a person.

Did you choose your job because it was the right job for you? Or are you there because "I'm not smart enough" has locked you into a predictable career and life path?

Is your love life nonexistent because you're too busy with work, haven't met that special someone/anyone/ seriously-I'll-take-anything-that-has-a-pulse-and-can-talk, or because you have an underlying conclusion about not being attractive enough or "not wanted" or "not lovable?" Is your current relationship on the rocks because it's not a good fit or because your conclusions have been running all over it and you're continually picking that person to death to confirm your own subconscious reality?

It's hard to tell now, huh!?

What are the automatic, reactionary thoughts you have when you suffer setbacks in life? What popped into your head when you got fired from that job or passed over for that promotion?

What was on your mind when you broke up with your last girlfriend or boyfriend or when you let that someone down or spent that money you knew you should have saved or ate that bag of fries when you should have opted for the salad?

Again, set aside all the surface stuff. What do you say to yourself about *you* in those situations?

Okay. There yet?

Once this is absolutely clear for you, you have the first critical piece of this important jigsaw in place. One of the reasons you self-sabotage is inextricably linked to this piece. We are not going to do anything with this right now but rather post it here like a flag in the ground.

PERSONAL CONCLUSION—
"I'M _____."

Go ahead, write it in here. Use a pencil if you're too embarrassed to ink your innermost secret about yourself on the page of a book. No really, go get a pencil. I'll wait right here.

People often ask me how I've been able to be successful without sabotaging my life, to maintain balance and be joyful while continuing to create health challenges and goals.

This is how. I am crystal clear about what I have concluded about myself.

What that thing is, how it feels, how it influences my moods and my outlook and the potentially devastating impact it can have when left to rampage its way through my life like Mad Max on steroids when I'm not on top of it. When I'm not being responsible for my default, most ordinary self.

I have awareness of this mechanism, and that awareness allows me to live a life outside of its grip. I can hear myself when I'm deep in it; I am intimately aware of the thoughts, the emotions surrounding it; I can actually feel this thing in a physical sense when I am about to go down the rabbit hole with it.

You can too, but we're not there yet. We have work to do that will allow you to master the unseen and finally take your life back.

> "Every man takes the limits of his own field of
> vision for the limits of the world. This is an error
> of the intellect."
> —Arthur Schopenhauer

ONE DOWN, TWO TO GO

Now we have something to build upon, to start to make you fully aware of and responsible for what has been lurking in the shadows of your subconscious. But we're not done yet. Far from it. There's more to this picture that you need to uncover for yourself.

Get your nose out of your belly button and look out around you. You live this life not on your own but with . . . ?

PEOPLE!

You share your life with people! That includes the people you don't talk to anymore. Remember those people, the ones you melted away from or cut out, the ones who still leave a little bit of an open wound in your mind? Yes, you are still sharing your life with them too. I mean, you might not speak with them, you might not have seen them for five, ten, or twenty years, but they continue to exist in your internal and external dialogues. They come up from time to time, either in spoken conversations or in the ones you have with yourself.

Look, they're even "here" right now—you have them *in mind*!

Even if you consider yourself a complete loner, you get to be a loner only against the backdrop of other people. Even your privacy is public. You are publicly private. Privacy is a very public statement to others. To keep out, to stay back.

"Dammit!"

I know, you thought you were doing so well with your reserved and withheld self too, didn't you? Sorry, but everyone is watching.

The next step as we fill out this picture of yourself is that you'll need to do some work to unveil what you have concluded about people. Not just some people. All people.

09

Them

It takes as
much effort
to live a crappy
life as it does
a great one.
And you're the
only one who
can choose
which you
want to live.

The first of the three saboteurs, your conclusion about yourself, is, unfortunately, just the first piece of this unholy trinity that leads to self-sabotage.

> *"The little world of childhood with its familiar surroundings is a model of the greater world. The more intensively the family has stamped its character upon the child, the more it will tend to feel and see its earlier miniature world again in the bigger world of adult life."*
> —C. G. Jung

The second saboteur is what I call your "social conclusion," or the fundamental lens through which you see and interact with *other people.* Like your personal conclusion, this was absorbed into the magic little sponge at an early age too. However, this baseline criticism about other people arose through your various interactions with your family, your friends, and your neighbors, as well as with teachers, pastors, and anyone else of significance with whom you came into contact in the formative years of your life.

From all of those life experiences, THIS is what you have concluded about other people. This is who they are for you. Again, not who they actually are or who they could be but rather who they definitively are to *you.*

The most important thing to get here, like everything else in this book, is that this is not something that was done to you. You're not a victim of your own past. I'm not saying people don't *become* victims to their past; I'm saying you are not one until the moment in time you decide you are.

If that annoys you, just realize you're currently getting triggered by your insistence on being called a victim. You are fighting for a label you're going to spend a lifetime trying to get over. Victim or no victim, only you get to say. In this case, you and you alone have made your life what it has become. Again, this isn't about who is to blame but is rather a way of you finally understanding yourself that empowers you rather than embitters or hardens you.

The good news is, if you accept that you made the mess, you are also accepting that you can unmake it. I often have to remind people of their power. It takes as much effort to live a crappy life as it does a great one. And you're the only one who can choose which you want to live.

Your social conclusion is the perfect mode of survival. Remember, we're all striving for safety and security in life, and other people are one of the least predictable parts of life! By coming to conclusions about people, we bring a feeling of certainty to the great unknown and threat that people represent.

Unfortunately, you're often focused on surviving events in life that just don't need to be survived!

Sometimes you're worried about "making it" in a relationship, or on a first date, or when speaking to people at a meeting, or calling up your credit card company, or talking to the leadership group on a conference call, or facing the prying eyes and ears at a wedding, or standing in line at the supermarket. You're stuck in a swirl of your automatic instinct to survive some old thoughts and emotions. But do you really need to be in survival mode about those things? You're stuck on surviving what you concluded about people. And it's all so fucking real.

So, what do these social conclusions look like? In the previous chapter, we touched on the inherently negative nature of conclusions. We saw this to be true when it comes to the negative conclusions we land on about ourselves. And it's the same for the conclusion you've made up about other people.

This is stuff like "People are controlling" or "People can't be trusted." In reality, all it takes is one or two life incidents for these conclusions to seep into that magic little sponge of yours. And as we all know, there are plenty of things that interrupt the innocence of a childhood, from the particularly shitty—maybe you were beaten, molested, neglected, or ignored—to the mundane. No matter the severity, we all have conclusions that run deep. Keep in mind, whatever you resist about your life persists by virtue of that resistance. You are swamped by your conclusions in the same way everyone else is by theirs.

I've also had many clients over the years who had *seemingly* idyllic childhoods and could not understand why their adult lives had gone so spectacularly off the rails. Until I introduced them to their own conclusions.

God forbid that your parents might have been lost in the escapism of the TV when you were pleading for their attention or drove off into the distance with you far behind, still screaming in the arms of the babysitter! You can see why being separated from Dad in a department store for just a minute or two could start to give rise to the kind of profound conclusion that eventually embeds itself into your young and eager subconscious. How easily that one incident could soak into your magic little sponge and become "People will leave," "You can't trust people," or "People don't care." Thereafter follows a lifetime of gathering evidence to support your view.

What!!?? That's all it takes? Being separated from your dad for a few minutes in a store? It can be, yeah. At least that's how it can start. It doesn't take a *Flowers in the Attic* childhood to produce a mad, mad, mad world kind of adulthood!

Once those conclusions are made, you're a done deal. That little sponge eventually hardens when the wispy, watery memories disappear, leaving only the stains and marks trapped inside, forever. Trapped in your subconscious. No amount of fucking existential Goo Gone can wipe that clean. You can't meditate your way out of it, either.

This takes a self-realization, a WTF kind of awakening, just like old Ebenezer had.

As we move on to adulthood, these conclusions stick with us, forming the baseline for how we relate to and interact with everyone we meet. And I mean *everyone*.

We're constantly viewing the people around us through the lens of these conclusions.

> *Meanwhile, we're manipulating and shaping ourselves—how we act, talk, dress—to keep people from exposing our most painful truth, that which we have concluded.*

We do this because for each of us, these conclusions, these saboteurs, would make us seem weaker or unwanted by the larger group, so we hide them.

THROUGH THE FILTER THEY GO

As with the previous saboteur, the conclusion about yourself, let's make this real for you. When I say that we view people through the perspective of our conclusion, what we're also doing is testing them to see how they measure up to what we've concluded. Do they conform? Do they conflict?

As an example, let's say you have the conclusion "People will use you." Whether you realize it or not, you are constantly running the people you meet through your internal filter to see if they fit the "Are they a user?" bill.

Always at arm's length, of course.

Did you catch them lying? Oops, they fail the test. "Are they *really* trying to flatter me in exchange for a favor?" Fail. "Talking behind my back?" Another fail. That voice in your head is in a constant state of judgment and pass/fail.

Hell, you can always fall back on the "vibe" test. "There's something about them I just don't like." It's inescapable.

It's just so damn easy for people you've just met to fail and the ones you've known forever to keep failing. Your "pass or fail" mechanism is always on. You're like a permanently lit barcode scanner at Target. Beep, beep, fucking beep. No one. Stands. A. Chance.

And once something sets off that little scanner, you go right into autopilot, gathering more evidence that puts that person further and further in the hole. Once you get your evidence, you write them off completely. Then they're really fucked. The problem is, so are you.

Because once you write someone off, you're going to ride that train until the end. There's almost nothing that can get them back in your good graces, barring a miracle or cataclysm. They're in the box, trapped, never to be released. Whether with your family, friends, acquaintances, and strangers or in your love relationships, that trigger, that fundamental conclusion about people, is there. Unfortunately, you are as trapped by your own conclusion as they are. You get to know and receive people only at that surface level.

But some people still manage to pass the test. The ones who "passed" are the people who are in your life now—at least the ones you're closest with.

Your best friends, they're in, your spouse or partner, they're in (for now), and you probably have some acquaintances who haven't quite passed, but they haven't quite failed either. Arm's length would be the best way to describe those relationships. Neither in nor out, but you never know, they might come in handy in the future.

And even with these people who somehow manage to pass your test, approved by your filter, they are forever skating on thin ice. Because you know it takes only one meaningful incident for them to go right back into the failure pile.

But for all the others who didn't pass the test, they were written off. Out.

Often family are the first to go. The writing-off process is a little different for everyone. Some of us just write people off silently over a period of time, within ever-decreasing circles of connection and affection. The death of love and affinity.

Sometimes the other person doesn't even realize it's happening, and often the person doing the writing off doesn't either! But there are subtle clues (that make sense later) in how we act around them. It starts with being a little slower than usual in responding to texts or phone calls until we eventually just stop communicating and reorganize our lives to avoid them.

Of course, then there are those relationships that are killed off in an instant.

The problem with all of this is that you're never quite seeing people for who they *truly* are or even who they *could* be. You're seeing them only through the lens of your own conclusion. The test isn't fair. They're set up to fail.

Don't even get me started with how you've collected agreements from certain friends while huddled around your chai lattes and orange muffins or clasping your ever-so-well-branded Heineken with your crew. "But they *agree* that my boss is the worst!" They're not only confirming your conclusion; it's all fucking gossip too. While we're at it, cut that shit out too.

> *Gossip is not fucking harmless or funny. You're peddling in negative, self-righteous BS. Stop talking about other people. It's a distraction from owning and changing your own life.*

Remember, you are the *nature* of what you talk about.

When you indulge in gossip, you are becoming the kind of human being who gets off on throwing other human beings under the bus. You might want to consider new friends or starting a revolution of bare-bones decency and engaging in the kind of talk that makes things happen rather than the kind that just shreds others in that shallow connection of human asshole-ness.

I'm also not a blind idealist here. I know people do shitty things. I am well aware that people will cheat, lie, manipulate, steal, and do whatever they feel is in their best interests, regardless of the cost. That's not what this is about. This isn't about payback. This isn't about them. This is about you.

Payback? I don't have enough time for that shit. If you're making your life about payback, that's NOT karma. That's being angry and spiteful and vengeful.

Karma doesn't take sides.

You might find that a painful discovery of your own one of these days when indulging your retribution. Resentment is a burden you bear on your own. Sure, you might make that "okay," like all the other BS in your life, but be left in no doubt, the burden is real and it weighs you down in ways you can't even imagine.

What's the alternative? Well, for a start, I don't tolerate other people's bullshit. That's on them. I don't waste my life hanging onto their shit either. I'm up front, judgment-free, authentic, and open. When I say "judgment-free" I really mean that. I'm in no place to judge anyone in this life; everyone has their own choices to make. I do, however, get to say how this goes.

If you wanna hang with me, here's the rules. If you don't, I got it. When you're ready, here's where I am. If you're never ready to play that way: Oh well. To each their own. It's all meaningless anyway. Ten, twenty, or fifty years from now, barely anyone will even remember you were here, let alone which upsets you devoted your life to.

Whatever someone else does to you, it doesn't mean you automatically change who you are, because when you do, you become a smaller human being. You become a lesser version of yourself when you get angry because of their anger or resentful because of their resentment.

Your love, your self-expression, are there to be broadcast to the world, not shut down, manipulated and controlled in the ruins of a once blooming friendship or relationship. Resentment is for fools and the unaware.

Forgiveness, love, and connection between you and other human beings is where it's at. I know that's not always easy, but that is your job. Work it out. Work out how to be that kind of human being. That doesn't make you a doormat either.

We've all done things in our lives that just don't work, things that have eventually worked against us; I'm not judging you for what you might have done in the past either. I'm calling you out on who you have been turning *yourself* into before it's too late. Wake up.

WELCOME TO THE JUNGLE

I'll let you in on something.

The subconscious conclusion I made about people is that "people don't care." As in, the people around me (and people in general) really don't give a shit about anyone but themselves. And sure, this may be somewhat true for a lot of people, but not to the level I've elevated it in my subconscious.

It's automatic for me now. This is my social conclusion, the second of my three saboteurs. It's what immediately comes up in my moments of pressure or duress or conflict. It's sometimes ugly and greasy and in complete contrast to my commitment to people. It's the constant invisible wall between me and others.

It also colors my approach to many aspects of my life in a very singular way. From driving, to going to the mall, to watching TV, all of it. Again, I'm not walking around the mall like a raging lunatic, but just because the flag isn't flying, it doesn't mean there's no danger lurking.

I'll give you an example.

Not too long ago, my wife and I ordered a sofa. It was a pretty big sofa. And when I had it delivered, the movers decided it'd be a good idea to drop it off right at the end of my driveway. Great, right? Apparently, as my wife likes to remind me to this day, I didn't check the right box when we ordered it. So, there's this giant fucking sofa wrapped in plastic sitting sixty feet from my front door like the rotting carcass of a once-frozen mammoth uncovered in the middle of some distant tundra.

While some people might have asked for help, in my mind "people don't care," so therefore knocking on the neighbors' door and asking for a hand simply wasn't an option. It didn't even occur to me that I should or even *could* do that. It just wasn't on my radar! There was no process of should I or shouldn't I; it was automatic and instant. I mean, no one gives a fuck about me and what I have to deal with, right? God forbid they might say no or get annoyed or bothered by my intrusion.

I wasn't methodically going through this internal mental processing at the time. I'm now conditioned to live this way. It happened in seconds, and in the moment I did what I would always do.

I did it myself.

I wrestled that giant turd up the driveway, through a door opening clearly designed for prepubescent Hobbits shuffling in single file, then through two child gates that would put Israeli airport security to shame, and through *another* doorway custom-built for an eight-foot walking pencil. Finally, I bundled it arse-over-elbow into the desired room like one of those *Fast and the Furious* stunt cars spinning into a parking space facing the wrong direction at eighty-seven miles per hour.

Like I said, this was a big sofa, but with a smattering of low-frequency grunts, a lathering of elbow grease, MacGyver-style imagination, and nuclear-ground bursts of profanity, I managed to eventually do it.

My wife stood there, hands on hips, with that "You're an idiot" loving glare that she has come to master over many years of witnessing my special kind of madness.

This is the kind of shit your saboteurs drive you to. They shape how you participate in life. Of course, some of you are probably thinking I'm insane—while there are others who are sitting there reading this, nodding their head and wondering what the problem is here.

You know exactly where I'm coming from.

At a really fundamental level, this makes complete sense to the way that I see life. I'm independent. Sometimes catastrophically so. In an I-don't-really-need-people kinda way. On one hand, that independence works for me. As an author, I need to be self-generative and can generate a steady perseverance without outside influence or coaxing.

Then there's the ways that it works against me (particularly when furniture is involved), like how easy it could be for me to do this life alone and the impact choosing independence would have on my marriage or my kids. It's not vindictive—I mean, I love people—but in my mind, I just don't *need* them.

Those who are slavishly independent will testify to the ravenous appetite for that singular way of living. Many of you have had a trail of broken relationships, of being constantly unsettled and striving to feed that beast. Then there's the loneliness . . . the cold, unforgiving disconnect of loneliness.

Independence has become the answer, but not always to the question that is being asked.

THE ROOT OF HOW YOU FEEL ABOUT PEOPLE

I've talked about the necessity of uncovering the conclusions we made about ourselves, and it's equally as important to do the same for the one you made about other people.

But if this is buried deep in your subconscious, how exactly do you do that? Let's get personal and spend the next few pages figuring out what your hidden conclusion about others is.

Start with thinking about the times when you make conscious excuses for your unconscious thought processes. Those excuses are another hint toward your conclusion. Try to be aware of when you make those excuses and catch yourself doing it. But I'm not talking about legitimate excuses for legitimate problems. I'm talking about when parties, nights out, and dinner with "friends" feels like the equivalent of sunlight to a vampire. Or when someone proposes a business idea and you immediately think of all the ways they will try to fuck you over.

Perhaps you have a particular label that you assign to people with certain qualities, traits, or talents that you automatically avoid. Your conclusion might well be right underneath that little thing that irks you so much. Are they too smart? Does that make them arrogant or dominating to you? Do you avoid those people? What does that say about them?

Are they too "polished" or "together" in a way that makes them seem selfish? Perhaps they're too outgoing, which points to their aggression or insensitivity?

What is the common denominator, the all-pervasive conclusion, that allows you to predict and make sense of people?

Set aside your usual BS, scratch at the surface of your thoughts, tell yourself the truth. What are you *really* trying to avoid about people? People are what?

This second saboteur, your conclusion about others, could be anything: People are . . .

- stupid
- untrustworthy
- a threat
- unreliable
- uncaring
- selfish
- cruel
- manipulative
- untrustworthy

Which one captures your baseline experience of people? It might be none of the above, but these are just some samples of what it could be for you. The real question is, what's yours?

Keep in mind, the nature of this conclusion, like all of the three saboteurs, is that of a criticism. In this case, your grievance with other people.

Don't move on until you find the phrase that resonates with you, the one that truly captures your experience of people—all people.

You know the drill. Get a pencil or pen and fill in the blank.

SOCIAL CONCLUSION–
"PEOPLE ARE _____."

Remember, this isn't just an opinion of people. This is what you have fundamentally concluded about human beings. Once you've filled in this blank, keep in mind that first saboteur, your personal conclusion. We're building a picture, and we're almost there.

It's time to move on to the final saboteur, the conclusion you've made about life itself. We all have a certain angle on life; it appeals to each of us in a very fundamental yet personal way. Sure, we've all heard people say things like "Life is an adventure" or "Life is amazing," but what if we were to dig a little deeper? What's down there, trapped in the magic little sponge, defining how we feel about life?

Buckle up. This one is a doozy, folks.

10

Life

We rewrite our dreams or stuff them away in the darkness to avoid having them shattered. We keep them tucked away. For hope. For later. Maybe. We trade them in for a life less lived.

Got your conclusion about yourself? Check. Your conclusion about other people? Check. Then it's time to move on to our final saboteur, which many people feel is often the heaviest of them all.

This is the conclusion you've made about life itself. How do you *feel* about life?

I don't mean just *your life*. Life. The whole thing, all of it. What stirs for you when you take a look at where you're at, including all of the family and relationship stuff, what's going on with your work, your neighborhood, your town. Take it out even further to social issues and political concerns you have, the problems and tragedies currently facing the country and the world.

This life thing is massive and complex and unpredictable and at times completely overwhelming.

It's no wonder we are becoming more and more addicted to positive attitudes or freeing ourselves from our earthly pursuits in favor of something a little more experiential. A little longer lasting. A bypass for the strains of daily life.

If you follow me online, you already are aware of my aversion to positivity. It's like a fucking disease spreading through society like wildfire. I mean, I have nothing against being positive per se, but the addiction to it crushes everyone else who isn't quite so effortlessly sprinkled with the magic yay-dust. It can be a bit too much at times to be told to keep your chin up when your relationship to yourself is so dire! I've also met far too many positivity-heads who became so encumbered by their sugary goodness that they ignored or lived in complete denial of the gravity of their situation. Until it was much too late.

Heck, if we *really* believed that life was wonderful and absolutely filled with possibility, we wouldn't have to say it. We wouldn't need reminders or memes on social media to keep us in check. It would be like gravity, just *there* all the time, so much so that, like gravity, we wouldn't even notice it. And it's not. So, what is there instead?

But we almost have to tell ourselves the upbeat, positive story that life is this way or that to distract us from what we really believe to be true.

Deep down in your subconscious, there resides a life conclusion:

"Life is hard."
"Life is complicated."
"Life is a struggle."
"Life is too much."

Like the rest of your conclusions, it's never good news!

In fact, while what you think about yourself and others might upset you, what you think about life is what *really* puts the lid on everything.

> *"Every man has some reminiscences which he would not tell to everyone, but only to his friends. He has others which he would not reveal even to his friends, but only to himself, and that in secret. But finally there are still others which a man is even afraid to tell himself, and every decent man has a considerable number of such things stored away."*
> —*Fyodor Dostoyevsky*

A LIFE WITH CONSEQUENCE

Without your even realizing it, your conclusion about life shapes and influences the everyday paths you take and burdens you to live with the consequence.

If you've concluded that "life is a struggle," you're going to work hard to overcome that struggle with all the positivity or hard work or logical thinking that you can muster, but you'll inadvertently be making sure it stays one too. You'll pass up or write off opportunities and openings for change that seem too easy or too complex, or you'll sabotage yourself when you're seemingly winning.

Right back into the struggle you'll tumble.

How many times have you thought, "If I could just stop eating this" or "If I could just stop spending money on that," but you keep doing it anyway?

Rather than avoid the struggle, you literally keep yourself in it. You make the same mistakes again and again, hit the same pitfalls over and over.

Many of our problems in life could be solved fairly simply, but we somehow can't, don't, or won't deal with them. You need to look past the litany of ready-to-hand explanations here.

It's what you have concluded about life that has you stuck in a certain place.

You might be someone who is driven by the conclusion "Life is hard." From the outside, you're doing great! You have a dream job or business or family. But you're aware of something else, something that pulls you down most days. But still you work hard at it, you persevere, and you have your victories here and there.

But those great circumstances are fleeting. It eventually always ends up "hard," doesn't it? Too many emails, too many meetings, too many complaints from your partner or kids or parents or friends. Not enough time or money or knowledge or whatever.

What you're dealing with internally often doesn't match up to what is going on externally.

Even though this life you have built was supposed to be the answer to the life you used to have.

On the other hand, your life might have very little by way of positive circumstances in it. You might really feel as if you're on the bottom, and even your hard-earned shots at success in the past eventually turned in that predictable direction.

Listen, you might be living your life on the thinnest of edges, existing each moment no more than a hair's breadth away from crying or getting angry or collapsing into hopelessness, day after day after day. You can't talk to anyone about it because you've built a facade of keeping your shit together, you believe no one can help you, and you've finally succumbed to the daily one-more-drink answer to pull yourself back from the brink of yet another fall into the valley of your hapless, hopeless misery.

You're on the run, but you can't run anymore. You're out of breath, out of ideas, and the walls are closing in on you. As we learned in the previous chapters, we are so uncontrollably driven for our conclusions to be vindicated. We need them to resonate and provide some solid foundation to an otherwise willowy, uncertain existence, but when is this fucking madness going to end?

You don't have problems! You have *your* problems! The perfect issues, specific to you, that allow you to continue with this daily absurdity. And that's what it is. Absurd. Your whole fucking life is absurd now.

All because you've told yourself that life can't be any different from what you have come to believe.

SNATCHING DEFEAT FROM THE JAWS OF VICTORY

You might have read a book or listened to a seminar and thought, "Aha! I can finally make sense of myself." You got hold of something about yourself that resonated and made a difference at the time. But does it really get to the heart of you and why you are the way you are? Probably not.

That's more than likely because you're always stuck with that conclusion you've made about life.

You might consciously think you're sorted out, but those subconscious conclusions have different plans. And eventually, they prevail. Every time.

When you do experience a victory, it's a victory against your conclusions. When you get a promotion at work or build a successful business, that's not a victory in your career or your finances—it's a victory against what you've subconsciously determined about how "life is a struggle" or "life is unfair." You feel good! Your future looks brighter, and your current life is syncing up nicely with it. Then shit happens and down you go. Back your conclusion comes. "See? Life really is unfair, or else I wouldn't have gotten fired. When am I ever going to catch a break?"

In fact, when you strategize to make something good happen in your life, you're doing that precisely because of your conclusions. If you didn't fundamentally believe "life is hard," you wouldn't need to do what you do to make your life work. You could just sit on the couch all day watching TV or your plants grow or your favorite undies splashing around in the washing machine like they're on vacation.

> "Through pride we are ever deceiving ourselves. But deep down below the surface of the average conscience a still, small voice says to us, something is out of tune."
> —C. G. Jung

Have you ever felt like you're so close to success that you can see the light at the end of the tunnel, only to have that success slip between your fingers? What if that was supposed to go that way because that particular success would have been a threat to what you have fundamentally concluded?

The moment before you cross the finish line, you fall. Or you stop running. Or you get absorbed in something else, something shinier or better or bigger. The dark arts of distraction take over.

Right at the brink of success, there's this nagging dialogue in our subconscious saying, "Wait, this isn't right. Life is a struggle, it can't be this easy, there has to be something else." And we stumble and fall. Or sabotage.

We ask ourselves, "Is this it? I can't be fulfilled, because life is unfulfilling." Or unfair or dangerous or a disappointment. Whatever your fundamental "life is" might be.

There's a glass ceiling that you can't see, that sends you right back down to earth the moment you try to surpass it. And when you bump your head on that ceiling and your ass hits the floor, you've once again proven your conclusion about life.

You can improve yourself, get smarter and stronger and more secure, but you can never get past that conclusion. The experiences of improvement and success are fleeting.

Of course, there are the people on the other end of the spectrum. We saw that a certain type of person tries to overcome their conclusion that "life is hard" by working extra hard to outrun it. But there are other people with the same conclusion who respond by giving in to it. Hey, maybe living in a tent in the middle of nowhere isn't such a bad idea after all! Or they have conclusions that are so toxic, so limiting, that they don't even try. It's called "settling" for the life you have. It's when you become worn down, shaped, and limited by your internal dialogue to the point of surrender.

There are plenty of smart, capable people out there who fall way below their potential. And they know it. In a way, their intelligence or intuition can be a curse because it makes their conclusions even more real. They *know* they could be making a bigger difference, knocking this life out of the park, and yet they're stuck.

Why pursue your most extreme potential if "life is a disappointment"? Wouldn't you just be better off aiming a bit lower? Maybe a lot lower?

As they say, ignorance is bliss. And sometimes the most perceptive or intuitive of people can also be the most disillusioned and cynical. Their conclusions can have the most destructive of impacts and partner perfectly with the best, most compelling of excuses based upon apparently sound reason and logic. But they're still excuses.

Because, as with all of our other conclusions, we use excuses to cover our reality. We explain our lives. Again, that's the problem with excuses. They don't seem like excuses at all. At least not to the bearer.

Consider this. There are people who say "Money is the root of all evil," "Money doesn't buy you happiness," or something similar. Maybe they go so far as to give up their job, their education, their home, and so forth, to live a life that's less materialistic.

And sure, there's a lot to be said about avoiding the pitfalls of consumerism and materialism and the pursuit of happiness through accumulation.

But how many people have done the work to see if they *truly* believe their own view? How many of them settle for their explanation to themselves, one that they've had so long and believe without question, without introspection? What if they are actually avoiding something? Perhaps what they are *really* doing is trying to steer clear of the complexity or hassle or burden or stress or morality that they associate with becoming successful or making money. Or even avoiding the chance, God forbid, that they might fail, publicly, for all to see?

I can't pretend to know what everyone is thinking, but I'm certain that plenty of the people who don't "want" to be rich would happily accept that million dollars or two if you handed it to them. Now, if you haven't guessed already, this isn't about the money; this is very much about beginning to stare your own "truths" in the face. Elements of your own life that you've lived with but rarely, if ever, questioned. This could apply to certain career, life, or personal accomplishments or milestones, all the way down to finally accepting something that you've built a body of evidence to resist, and all driven by something you concluded many, many moons ago.

> "The reasons and purposes for habits are always lies that are added only after some people begin to attack these habits and to ask for reasons and purposes."
> —Friedrich Nietzsche

WELCOME TO THE JUNGLE

I had a client who discovered her conclusion was "Life isn't fair." Over the following weeks and months, she pulled at that thread of justice and fairness that had weaved its predictable way through her life. She uncovered the friendships that had become fractured by it, the bosses she had alienated, her chaotic relationships with family, and her constant experience of a life she perceived as unjust.

Her marriage had faltered and ultimately died from the daily bickering and contention about who was right and what was fair in that relationship. It was no longer about love or connection or passion but rather about what was equitable. It was the lens through which she saw her entire life, and, of course, her view was not just a view. It was *the truth*. At least, her truth.

Imagine that life. Imagine starting every day from a view that life itself is fundamentally unfair. How could that not taint your experience of being alive? You're already a victim in that scenario. You don't need tragedy or mishap; you can find it everywhere. It's all around you!

For me, I have seemingly built my life on my work ethic—but there are days when I'm just so burnt out. And all from my conclusion that "life is a struggle." Just as it is for you, my conclusion doesn't just seem like a noise in my head. It's so goddamn *real*! That "struggle" is as tangible for me as my hair.

In my case, that conclusion drives me to fight harder and harder. Imagine what it's like going on vacation with me! I wander around looking for things to *do*. There's no relaxing, there's no peace. I'm restless, uneasy, itching for something, *anything*, to allow me to engage with the struggle that life has become in my own mind.

On the journey home from any vacation, it's already kicking in. I cannot wait to go back into the fire of that hard, hard work, like that's going to get me out of "this struggle." Except it never does. It just perpetuates it. Keeps it going. Life really does become the struggle I have concluded. Even when it's good, it's a struggle.

Don't get me wrong. I, like you, have my days, plenty of them, when the birds are singing, my lungs are filled with optimism, and my actions are fueled by the hunger for the game. But that bottom line, the place from which it all starts, is never far away: perhaps in an hour or in the afternoon or tonight or when I wake up tomorrow.

No wonder we're so thirsty for motivation. It's hard to stay motivated when you think that life is a never-ending struggle. Sometimes it's like "What's the point?" Sometimes it's easier to just say "Fuck it" and subconsciously resign ourselves to where we're at in life. To surrender.

We rewrite our dreams or stuff them away in the darkness to avoid having them shattered. We keep them tucked away. For hope. For later. Maybe. We trade them in for a life less lived.

Your life conclusion will do that, by the way. It eats away at your experience of being alive. It burdens and dominates what you see as possible. When you awake, you step into an already existing reality. Your reality. Your conclusion. Life is . . . what?

TAKING A LEAP IN CONCRETE BOOTS

If you want to eventually get to exist beyond your own conclusion about life, you're going to have to figure out what it is first. And now is the perfect time to do so.

This can be tough because these life conclusions are often the least obvious. They're so pervasive, they're so soaked into every part of our lives, that it's hard to pinpoint exactly what they are.

It seems to me the most important thing to uncover is the nature of this conclusion rather than specifically what it is. There's not much difference between "Life is hard" and "Life is a struggle." They both would have a similar effect on how one interacts with life. It's the same with "Life is dangerous" and "Life is threatening." Again, you would have a very specific outlook, with these sentences working you in the background like an amateur ventriloquist's sweaty hand.

But there are times when we can catch a glimpse, when it's closer to the surface.

When you're pressed in life, when you're struggling every day or every week, one or all of your conclusions will be in your face.

What is it you say to yourself *about* life when it's not going your way?

When you're having a hard time is when you're most wrapped up in your conclusions about one area . . . or sometimes all.

When you're up to your throat in it, these conclusions wash over you when you're losing or failing or rejected or just not making it.

They kick in when it's getting "too good" or too uncertain or getting you into an area of life that would require some significant reinvention. And so . . . you return to base. To the familiar. You sabotage and turn back.

Give particular attention to those times when you're stressed out or discouraged. What are the familiar, patterned thoughts that pop into your head during those times?

If you're not feeling that way now, think back to the last time it happened, the last time when you experienced being beat down or pressed. Perhaps you can think back to a time in your past, like your childhood, when you went through struggle, hardship, or danger, and that became the overarching or most influential experience of your young life. What did you conclude? Maybe your parents divorced, or your mom died, or you were held back a grade, or you never made the soccer team, and suddenly your idea of what life is started to change.

Your childhood was peppered with the kinds of events that inadvertently steered your younger self toward a life that has some kind of flavor to it, some kind of meaning that you happened upon and bled into the deepest crevices of that magic little sponge, to be used for future guidance. What is life to you? Perhaps it's "confusing" or "dangerous" or "too much" or "pointless."

Finally, look at the things you want in life but that you either don't pursue or always seem to fall short of.

For instance, what's your current dream life? Moving to Bali or Kansas or Dublin? Is it about being thinner or taller or richer? Does it include a house or a certain car or a certain body shape? No matter what it is, it's important for you to take note that even your dreams are lived within a certain range. They're certainly not limitless. Where is your starting point? What problem does that "dream life" solve that's at the low end of the range you exist in?

Don't settle for the surface-level explanations and excuses you've come up with. Dig deeper.

> *"Your perception will become clear only when you can look into your soul."*
> —C. G. Jung

That's where you'll find the conclusions you've made, the limitations you've placed on yourself. And you can do this for everything from your income to your relationships to your health to your hobbies to the age you want to retire.

These conclusions have bled into every element of your life, influencing both the paths you take and the paths you don't. It's important for you to take some stock here, to get in touch with your innermost fears and concerns. To allow yourself to slip down into the depths of your own struggle. Not to indulge it or embellish it, but to witness it. To see it do its thing. I want you to become the observer rather than the indulger. The eyewitness rather than the victim. Step way back from the *Days of Our Lives* drama of your sabotage and do some thinking. Piece this little mystery together for yourself.

Listen, you have made a damning conclusion about life. It's right in front of your face. This doesn't need to be solved but rather spoken into existence. It needs to rise from the muddled background of your thoughts, up through your consciousness, and out of your mouth. You need to say it out loud.

Life is . . .

Go grab that pen or pencil.

LIFE CONCLUSION—
"LIFE IS _____."

> "We forge the chains we wear in life."
> —Charles Dickens

I invite you to pause now. Take a moment and ponder what we have uncovered here. Not just your conclusion about life but the entirety of everything we've uncovered. It's important that you give yourself time to take stock, to let in what all of this means and what you have done with your life until now.

11

The Point
of the Spear

That's what true acceptance is for a human being. When you can let something be itself without any charge or reaction around that thing.

So far, we've uncovered the three kinds of conclusions, the three saboteurs that are indelibly marked on your subconscious. The source of your self-sabotage.

They're the all-consuming conclusions you've made about yourself, other people, and life itself.

I hope you've been able to bring your own conclusions to light, to do the critical thinking and figure out what they are and at least some of the ways they are keeping you stuck in this cycle of sabotage. In other words, it should be sinking in by now just how fucked you have really been, just like the rest of us!

The haze of "why" you undermine yourself should be beginning to lift. Remember, if certainty is key for a human being, then providing evidence for what you have already concluded is critical to that certainty. Your conclusions are your rock, the "truth" from where you can make sense of this world.

But where exactly does that leave you? Where does it locate you in this universe? In other words, when you put the three saboteurs together, what is your primary experience of being alive? That will be the final piece of the puzzle of understanding why you are the way you are, so that we can get to how to put self-sabotage to bed once and for all.

First, let's lay out what it's not. All of this doesn't add up to a unique point of view for you. That's way too simplistic. "Point of view" doesn't capture the gravity, the experience, and the all-encompassing restraint of what these conclusions are doing and where they are ultimately driving you. There's a way that being *alive* feels to you. THAT'S the point of the spear: what it's like for you to be alive.

That feeling, that experience of yourself, is where your conclusions combine to form a very personal *experience* of actually being you, something that permeates every part of your being.

It's not just the way you look at life—it's the place *from* which you engage with life. The way you hear it, see it, smell it, touch it, are inspired by it and deflated by it. A location from which you interact with everyone and everything you come into contact with.

Instead of a point of view, it's what I call your *point of experience*. The place from which you experience *everything*. Your distinct and unique starting point in life. No matter the future you are out to have, you are always starting from this same, familiar place, located by those three fundamental conclusions, your three saboteurs.

> *"Vision is the art of seeing the invisible."*
> —*Jonathan Swift*

FINDING YOURSELF ON THE MAP

You can picture this *point of experience* as your own little marker on Google Maps.

Every morning you wake up into a world.

As soon as your eyes open you are in a familiar location, and no, I don't mean in your bed. It's actually more like in your head! This isn't *the* world that greets you every morning but rather *your* unique world. A world filled with your nuances and triggers and biases from that distinct and unique point of experience that you have. You are completely shaped by those three saboteurs in a way that, until now, has been explained by you in terms of moods or emotions or behaviors or circumstances.

You've had those days when it's challenging to face the day or the week or that meeting or that email or that conversation. When you're up to your eyeballs in life and all the shit that comes with it.

Your life is a constant stream of same old, same old. No matter your dreams or hopes, it's all from the same self-imposed starting point, and that starting point isn't a starting point at all, really. You are in essence *always* behind, always at the bottom of the hill, always working your way up or toward a new goal or objective or outcome.

But what about the self-sabotage? Okay, steady yourself.

There are also those times when you get inspired by something—you fall in love with someone or get excited about a pay raise or a new job, or you get lit up by some new kind of opportunity for yourself. A new outlook emerges, and you're starting to feel pretty good about your life and where it's headed. In short, your present life is starting to echo with the life you want. It might not have all the pieces, but you're on track, right?

Maybe you're going to the gym regularly. It's been three weeks of effort, and you're feeling the difference.

Maybe you have stopped those self-destructive spending patterns and you've managed to keep an extra $20, $200, or $2,000 in your account. You're off to a great start, things are going to plan. It's going WELL!!

There's a little spring in your step, a tingle in your tummy, a glint in your eye, and then . . . uh-oh.

You take a day off from the gym. You spend a little of the money you've set aside. You start to question that new relationship, new job, or idea you had for a business. The deconstruct begins. Sometimes it's gradual; at other times, it's a full-scale assault on what you have built. You start to undo your progress.

BOOM!

This is the part where the old patterns, the familiar behaviors and emotions, start to take over, and all because you are now in unexplored territory.

Give this some thinking. If you are truly out to live a completely new life with a host of new results, could you live that new life as the same old you? NO!

Of course not, and that, my friend, is a problem. Why can't you? Because you are hardwired for safety, for your world to be a familiar and certain one. For the familiarity of those deep-seated conclusions no matter how unsavory or limiting they might be, to keep your existence connected to something, anything that you can make sense of, the kind of internal conundrum that supports you being distracted and occupied and ultimately lost in the safety of your own little reality.

Whatever new life you want for yourself requires you to *be* different. You can't be the same you you've always been, but at the same time you're also being pulled, dragged, and skewed by your three saboteurs, magnetically drawn back to that familiar point of experience. It just won't work. To authentically change your life requires you to authentically change yourself. A new life might require you to be more patient, more loving, more reliable, more bold, more vulnerable, more loyal, more focused or dedicated, more sociable, whatever the thing is: this new area will require you to *be* a different you! AND YOU CAN'T DO IT!!

That "new" you would be too uncertain, too risky, too overwhelming, too confusing and unnerving to face head-on.

So, what do you do? You revert to the starting point. You subconsciously blow it up. You undermine what you have built or aspired to so that life can go back to "normal," you can go back to being that old, familiar you and, after a while, begin the struggle all over again!

I mean, how many times have you cleaned your house or office or desk or garage, stood back and looked at the glowing magnificence of your cleaning skills, only to slowly witness it crumble under an avalanche of dirty socks, real estate flyers, and stuff you don't want to throw out but don't know what to do with?

You did it, cleaned it up, but you couldn't live that way, you couldn't sustain the kind of you who whipped that place into shape. You eventually surrendered to your default self.

Sabotage, baby.

That magic little sponge of yours, the home of your three saboteurs, is not so magic now, is it? It's hardened and coarse and impenetrable to anything new. Which means you're stuck, and stuck living out the same stale patterns day after day, year after year.

Are you starting to get the picture? Every day of your waking life you begin at a certain familiar *point of experience*, made up of those three saboteurs we talked about earlier. That's where they all come together to form your experience of being alive.

That point of experience isn't a comfortable, cozy place but rather a place you are out to improve, to make better, to eventually overcome and triumph over. That's why you live this "someday" kinda life, like one day this will all turn out, you'll have arrived, and everything will be awesome. Right?

Have you ever noticed how everything you are after is always *later*? It's never here, now. Even if that desired thing somehow does get accomplished, it gets replaced by another item or goal. So, you pursue that one now. Or you blow it up. Either way, it's the same shit, different day.

You think you are pursuing goals like more money, or a new career, or fame, or the love of your life. But that's an illusion.

As Sartre would have said, your life has been about "the pursuit of being." You are pursuing "being" a different you, the kind of you who solves the dilemma of the current you, to somehow relieve the weight of your point of experience. Those goals? They are what you *think* will make you different or better!

But that's the problem with pursuit. It's a constantly hungry animal. It requires prey, over and over and over. You have become addicted to the chase. That hunger to "be" a different kind of you is never satisfied.

Why? Because you cannot "have" being like a possession. It's un-have-able. You can't contain happiness or satisfaction or confidence in a jar. Those are all fleeting experiences of being alive. They rise and fall, show up and then recede, yet we still try to capture them! We try to make solid something that is inherently liquid. You, my insatiable friend, are an expression of being. Your authentic self-expression is a limitless broadcasting of what it is to "be." Yet you, like most human beings, rather than express happiness or love or passion, pursue those things with the idea that they are somehow attainable!

You are a human *being*. Yet you live as if you have some kind of limit or scarcity of *being*, and therefore you have become a human "doing"-to-eventually-"be."

That thing you are after, the target of that pursuit, you ALREADY ARE! Do you get the complete insanity of this? Why would you spend a lifetime looking for confidence or passion or love when these expressions already exist deep within you, with all of the majesty and power of the oceans and the mighty span and magnitude of an endless mountain range?

LEARNING TO TAKE THE BAD WITH THE WORSE

By now, you might be thinking, "Dammit, Gary! I get it, I have problems, I've lived my life in a dumb chase. Tell me the good news already!" Most of us want to skip the hard shit and jump straight to the good parts. I get no enjoyment from people's misery, but I haven't met a worthwhile transformation yet that didn't have some in it.

I want you to get better—but you need to stare this right in the eye. You need to look at what you have done (and are doing) with your life. The carnage of pursuit. The broken relationships, the failures, the regrets, the resentment, and yes, sometimes the despair.

Life isn't a movie, where the struggle and the happy ending are only an hour or two apart. And you can't fall asleep during the boring parts or cover your eyes when shit gets gory.

> "Impatience asks for the impossible, wants to reach the goal without the means of getting there. The length of the journey has to be borne with, for every moment is necessary."
> —Georg Wilhelm Friedrich Hegel

Putting Hegel in other words, the journey of this book itself is part of this process. You have to get in touch with what it's really like to be you, to be stuck in the grip of your conclusions, to fundamentally relate to being alive from your most basic point of experience. That's what we've been working at in these pages—getting you in touch with who you have become, deep down, and where you are coming from.

We try to placate our conclusions with our accomplishments. We try to get away from them with our progress. But that gives you momentary relief, at best. The conclusions are still there. You're still stuck at that same point of experience.

So, what can we do to get unstuck? Stop the striving and struggling, for starters, and just accept where you are. Be "here" for the moment. This moment. Attempting to overcome your point of experience is futile. You're trying to outrun a treadmill. You can't escape your conclusions by running. You can't out-think, out-hustle, or out-meditate this shit.

Many people spend half their life trying to overcome their conclusions, but they invariably end up back in the same place. That realization often whacks you upside the head by the time you're halfway through your thirties or forties.

Midlife crisis, anyone? It's that moment when you realize you're stuck. That you've been moving forward your whole life while staying in the same place. You notice that the point of experience is still there, and you're left with the question "Is this it, is this all there is?"

From your point of experience, yes, this is it, this is all there is. Most people do one of two things in this moment. Either they settle down to a quiet, suffocating surrender or they rebel and make a drastic life change. It's BS either way.

> "Aging people should know that their lives
> are not mounting and unfolding but that an
> inexorable inner process forces the contraction
> of life. For a young person it is almost a sin—
> and certainly a danger—to be too much

occupied with himself; but for the aging person it is a duty and a necessity to give serious attention to himself."
—C. G. Jung

There has to be a point in this book where you start to see your life up to the present moment. Look at the clock. What time is it? What's today's date?

Your entire life up until right now has been about surviving and pursuing and surviving and pursuing. Step back a moment. Look at your life as an observer. Be honest with yourself here. This is not a time for you to indulge your optimism or resignation or even your drama. Take stock of how this life of yours has been going, not just in one area but in the whole of it.

This will require you to put some space between yourself and what you are currently seeing here. There needs to be a gap where you can step back and look at this for yourself in the cold light of day. On one hand, there's you and this moment of time, and on the other is how your life has unfolded until now. Can you see it?

There has to be a real experience of you being able to observe your life from a distance instead of up to your back teeth in it.

No moving on until you have this down.

EMBRACING YOUR SHIT

Change begins with acceptance. Acceptance of what is already so. One cornerstone of Jung's theory of the mind is that you have to accept every part of yourself—the good, the bad, the light, and the dark.

What does genuine acceptance look like? Let's do a quick exercise.

Right now, think of something in your life that you barely, if ever, give thought to, something so mundane and benign it just fades into the background of your thoughts. It could be anything—the color of your car, your middle name, the light bulb above your head, the size of your feet. Any item that, when you give it some thought, has no impact on you one way or the other. You experience neither joy nor frustration nor sadness nor passion nor any emotional state connected to it. You literally experience *nothing* with regard to that item.

Do you know *why* that item has zero impact on you?

Because you genuinely accept that item the way it is. You have no urge for it to be better or different or for it to change in any way. You're not "past it" or "getting over it," and you have no need to cut it from your life or barely even think, let alone talk, about it.

And so, it sits there. Accepted. Undisturbed.

It has no bearing on you because you accept it for what it is. That item is itself, and while it's part of your life, it has no influence on you. There is no emotional tug at you.

That's what true acceptance is for a human being. When you can let something be itself without any charge or reaction around that thing. When it has no influence, and I mean NONE, good or bad. Nothing either way.

You can't ignore the darker parts of your unconscious. You can't repress them. Because they don't go anywhere. And oftentimes they just keep getting worse and emboldened by your attempts at having them go away or be somehow changed. Fueled by years of scratching that itch over and over and over. The basement of your mind is the perfect place for all your doubts and your fears to grow. Just as long as you keep giving them the sprinkle of daylight they need from time to time.

Until you accept them. Just right where they sit. In the dark.

Nothing to say about them, nothing to do with them other than let them be.

> "Unfortunately, there can be no doubt that man
> is, on the whole, less good than he imagines
> himself or wants to be. Everyone carries a

shadow, and the less it is embodied in the
individual's conscious life, the blacker and
denser it is."
—C. G. Jung

That's why we're going to stop running from our
conclusions, stop trying to overcome them through
denial, avoidance, or never-ending effort. Dig into
your conclusions. Investigate and explore them.
Uncover your point of experience on the map.

Let yourself be present to those days, weeks, months,
and years of self-sabotage, of the struggle to get
better, of temporary victories and mind-numbing
plunges into the depths of the darkness.

Let all of that up, sit in that stew . . . and then accept.

That's right, accept all of it. Realize that these
conclusions are only a part of you, not all of you. Make
peace with the fact that they're here to stay and that
your struggle to change them is what makes them play
such a big part in your life. Your unease has become
your disease.

Let it be, right here, right now. Just as it is.

*Acceptance is a practice. It's a
conscious exercise, a reminder—
sometimes daily, hourly, or by the
minute—to free yourself from your*

*automatic reactions and triggers, to
give yourself the space you need to
forge a life free of self-sabotage and
self-doubt.*

To begin living from the space granted by acceptance.

———————

You've been living on autopilot for most of your life.
What would it look like to be able to recognize and turn
that off? To wake up to your life? To feel fully alive?

If this life were no longer about you questioning your
intelligence or your capabilities, if people were no
longer a threat or controlling or untrustworthy, if life
weren't a struggle or a disappointment, how would that
change things? What kind of life could you take on?

Who could you be?

12

Redirecting Your Way Outta This

What are you
actually up to
that would make
this life of yours
a truly great one?

Finally, we are at the bottom.

We've come a long way from that magic little sponge, the life circumstances you were thrown into, your established truths, and the three saboteurs. Your point on the map is now clear. THAT'S the life you have. It's where you start every day, and it's ultimately where you are fated to return.

It's that repetitive, cyclical experience of yourself. The subconscious mechanism to keep life safe and predictable and survivable regardless of the cost to your aliveness or ambition.

This is why your life has been the way it has been. It stands to reason: if all of that is what got you to this point, it's the course your life will continue to take. Things might get better here and there, one thing or another will change, but the flavor of your life, the limits, the boundaries, the direction it's all headed, will continue.

But here's the thing you've *got* to understand. Where did you get this mechanism? It's all from the past. It was made in the past, forged in the moments of your life when you were forced to make sense of and survive a life that you were thrown into.

The reality is that every day is NOT a new day, because you are always starting from the burden of some of the earliest points of your childhood, continuing to act on those conclusions and carrying them into each day thereafter.

Your past dominates your potential. You don't live a life of "anything is possible"; you live a life of "some things are possible, given my past."

You're stunted, limited, a dreamer with no chance of breaking out of this self-imposed prison. Every day you begin from the past. Every idea, every hope, every plan, all of it, begins back there. Is it any wonder you never get anywhere? Your starting point is pushed way back, and you are irretrievably anchored to it.

> *"History repeats itself, first as tragedy, second as farce."*
> —*Karl Marx*

Earlier in the book when I said you're asleep? This is what I'm talking about! You're dozing off at the wheel of your life, maintaining a loop of the past. And at some level, you know it!

Everything you're trying to do is only to subconsciously prove the legitimacy of what you concluded, to return you to your point of experience and set you off in pursuit again. Your pointless diets, your awkward and hellish exercise regimes, your crappy relationships, your litany of financial disasters and splintered dreams, your job that no one else would do, let alone die for, your ever-dwindling ambition.

You.

And you are always winning. Even when you are apparently losing, it's a win for this cycle of BS.

You don't just have to overcome life, or the immediacy of your concerns; you have to overcome yourself—and not your best self but rather your worst, most negative, most cynical self.

It's as if you're trying to win a marathon but you're kicking off twenty miles behind everyone else. By the time you cross the starting line, the thing is almost over. Then back you go.

And that's what *all* self-help is trying to address, whether it's teaching you to set goals or do yoga or find your fucking purpose. It's what we're trying to change when we go on a diet, join a new gym, or start meditating. Every hope, every dream, every want, from that new car to that perfect partner or genius new business idea, it's all just the latest strategy to overcome *yourself.* To finally solve the problem that YOU are! A quick-fix trick to make you better at a game that is designed never to be won and is completely stacked against you. And yet you keep playing! To change something that's not changeable, and it's all a setup. You get swindled and then you die. That's how this goes.

STOP DOING THAT SHIT!! Wake up, you're in a trap!

It's what was sitting in the back of your mind when you decided to pick up this book. As if this would finally be the answer. There is no fucking answer!

So, what do we do with this thing that leads to our sabotage? Do we slay it? Fight it? Negotiate with it? Control it?

No. We do nothing. We do nothing with it. Let me expand this a little. Have you ever had a mosquito bite? Think about how itchy and annoying it is. You're just dying to scratch or squeeze or stick a rusty pin into it or do whatever you have to do to rid yourself of this infestation that occupies your peace of mind.

Now, you and I both know that the less you touch or think of the bite, the better it gets. At the same time, the more you focus on it, the itchier and more annoying it seems. In short, the more you resist and get consumed by that bite, the worse it gets.

Or think about it this way. If you have kids, you'll have done this. If you don't have kids, you might have seen a Jedi-mom pull this shit on your flight to Albuquerque last fall. It's called "redirection." When Mommy's (or Daddy's) little angel is starting to blow up like a two-foot volcano of venom, in steps the power of the redirect. Mom waves a toy, pulls out a magazine (a paper one, for the love of God), a piece of candy, or any mystery item at hand that could be spun into a dinosaur, wizard, giraffe, or Peppa Pig in an instant of imagination and pretend enthusiasm. Suddenly the gates to hell are closed and we're treated to the giggly oohs and aahs that we all love so dearly as that cherubic face abandons the blind fury of a misunderstood generation in favor of something a little more lovable. And the entire plane breathes a sigh of relief. To themselves, of course, because no one is going to publicly admit their cranky ass to a bunch of strangers, are they?!

What happens in that magical moment of redirection? First, the upset is left alone, not interrupted or shushed to death, not even acknowledged. Next, an entirely new and much more interesting item is introduced. In that very moment, the child's brain, like yours when focused authentically on something else, becomes so consumed by that new item that the other things seem to disappear from view. I call this an "authentic pivot." When you shift your attention to what genuinely interests, inspires, or invigorates you, whatever *was* on your mind, whatever direction you *were* headed, is now altered. You've authentically pivoted, and your mind, your actions, and your focus are now engrossed in what naturally lights you up.

Your life will go in the direction of whatever you give your attention, time, energy, and actions to, even if you mistakenly think that what you are doing will eventually fix the problem. Constantly trying to fix problems fills your life with . . . problems.

Whatever you resist persists, by virtue of your resistance, remember?

You've been living your life according to the past, but you now need to make the pivot to make your life about what's new, about your potential and your legacy. New emotional approaches, new behaviors, new habits, the kind of stuff that demonstrates the life you say you want.

WATTS THE CAUSE?

The British philosopher Alan Watts had an extraordinary view of our relationship with the past. He said, "In our ordinary common sense we think of time as a one-way motion from the past, through the present, and on into the future. And that carries along with it another impression, which is to say that life moves from the past to the future in such a way that *what happens now and what will happen is always the result of what has happened in the past.* In other words, we seem to be driven along."

Don't just read what he is saying like a one-and-done deal. Go back. Read it again until it makes sense to you. *Sit there for a moment and let the profundity of what this man is saying permeate your brain.*

What does all of that mean in the context of this book? It means you have lived your life, all of it, every minute, every hour, every day, as if everything you are doing or have done is *caused by*—is a result of—something that has already happened.

It means we have become accustomed, even addicted, to the notion that all we are and all we ever will be comes from who we have already been, and the absolute best we can hope for is to make who we have been, better! WHOA!

At the same time, *that* requires us to keep who we have been in existence! If who we have been no longer exists, there is nothing to improve, nothing to change, no day in the future when it will all work out. The ego eats itself. Over and over.

The cause of your existence is coming from the past into the present day and on into your future like a straight line.

Now, of course this is true! That's EXACTLY how you've lived your life up until this point! The past can be five seconds ago or five years ago, it's irrelevant, but you constantly use the past to explain why you are the way you are right now, whether you realize it or not. You justify by using the past. You excuse and explain by using the past. You plan for the future too by using the past as a template: what to do, what not to do.

Relationships are often built on not repeating the failures of past ones. Therefore, the limitations of those past experiences are brought into the next one as a measure or an ideal.

We raise our children in a way that we think will be better than our own childhoods. A future caused and shaped by the past. Sometimes a crappy past. Carried forward and caressed with all the tender care and attention of Gollum's alluring ring.

All of it, everything you do, is based in this hocus-pocus, this commonly accepted notion that we can only ever be a product of what has been.

For you, cause and effect travels in one direction only. A direct line of thoughts, emotions, experiences, and actions, started in the past and carried right through to today.

You stopped talking to your brother *because* of what he said six years ago, or you don't lift the phone to call your friend *because* of that thing she did last week, or you resist hanging out in large groups *because* of that thing that happened when you were twelve.

There are literally huge swathes of your life that you won't take on *because* of what has been.

What just happened is the cause of what's happening right now. What happened last year is the cause of this year. What happened when we were kids is the cause of our lives as adults. At least, that's how we've been trained to see it. It's fucking madness, and you've been suckered, brainwashed, compadre.

Watts continued, "So the whole idea of our being driven [in life] is connected with the idea of causality, of life moving under the power of the past. And that is so ingrained in our common sense that it's very difficult to get rid of it."

Wow!

So, what is the alternative? How do we make this life of sabotage obsolete? Well, there's clearly no way to go back and change the past. What happened back there is still what happened back there. The sponge is hard, stained, unchangeable. That goes for the conclusions you made. The past is in the past, that's it, done deal, and we cannot change it. So, let's leave that where it lies. Let's not touch it or engage with it. We can recognize it, we can accept it, and we can redirect in favor of something far more satisfying and filled with possibility.

Don't poke the fucking bear. Build a better model. A completely new design.

Which begs the question: If we really could build a new design, a new way of living, one that bankrupts our compulsion to self-sabotage, surely that would mean an end to looking to the past for guidance or insight? Abso-freaking-lutely it would!

Now, before you trot out one of the most abused phrases out there, "Those who do not learn from history are doomed to repeat it," I think we've proved without doubt we're on a one-way track of the same thing over and over and over. As a species, we must be one helluva slow burn when it comes to learning!

Of course, there are many things we can learn from our failures and tragedies. Obviously, we should be aware of danger or potential mishap when it presents itself, but at the same time, our past just doesn't apply to *everything* we are doing in our lives!

Then where should we look for guidance in the present moment?

The future, of course!

YOUR FUTURE SELF

Buckminster Fuller, the twentieth-century inventor and visionary, said, "You never change things by fighting the existing reality. To change something, build a new model that makes the existing model obsolete."

Now, those are some powerful words, my friend.

And that's exactly what we're going to do. Build something new. An entirely new approach to living your life.

We're going to make the past obsolete.

Instead of trying to fix the broken system, you have to create an entirely new one. One that will authentically pivot you in an entirely new direction. A bold and invigorating way for you to live your new life. This is the point in the book where you confront your way of living and the complete bankruptcy of your current method for "doing" life. That old way of life needs no more energy from you; in fact, it needs to be starved of attention and therefore life.

You need to be redirected. We're out to do something here that actually works. Something that pulls you toward your goals rather than conspiring against them. There's an energy, like a force of nature, between what you desire and where you are. But this force hasn't been helping you along. No, it has been pushing against you, pressing you back to where you came from, and that's why life changes can be so exhausting!

Your future has been anchored to the past. Period. Why? Because your entire life is modeled around either getting over the past or repeating it.

No wonder you give up or become resigned or succumb to the watery allure of being a victim.

THE FUTURE . . . IT'S NOT JUST STAR TREK

Before you start rolling your eyeballs so far back they never return, I'll lay this out for you.

I read somewhere recently that the TV series *Star Trek* predicted fifty advances in technology before they were invented, including tablet computers, GPS, automatic doors, cell phones, and teleconferencing. The list is quite impressive!

I'm certainly not out to just let this fact slip away and down into a potential topic for the next series of *Mysteries of the Universe* either! Nostradamus was NOT a scriptwriter for *Star Trek*!

Star Trek didn't *predict* anything. What planet are you on? *Star Trek created* something. The series was a product of the imagination, of the ability to think and conceptualize and visualize. Its creators didn't predict the future; they visualized one, a future that included some of those far-out technologies.

Okay, so what?

Well, those dreamt-up ideas inspired some people to see if they could actually work, people apparently energized by the possibility to such a degree that they started knocking those gadgets out like a cascade of Peanut M&Ms from the gaping mouth of a twenty-five-cent gumball machine!

Many of our modern-day advances are a product of people using their boldest, bravest imagination, sticking a flag in the ground, and then dealing with everything that comes up between here and that imagination being realized. They make their present about the future.

Dreams can easily become reality. Why can't someone use this approach to live a life to its fullest?

This isn't a new idea either. Major corporations design what's next all the time. They look to the future and make bold, unparalleled plans for investment or expansion or reinvention. They even set the date they intend to complete those unimaginable projects and brazen ideas. They then do something you and I don't do.

They work backward. Everything they do is guided *from* the future. They start with the ending! They begin to be shaped and informed by what's to come. Each new day is influenced by what hasn't happened yet! In a complete reversal of what Alan Watts said, rather than being driven from the past, corporations are being pulled by the future.

They start to have their vision for the future impact and influence their present. They are guided from the future, *caused* by the fucking future!

Holy shnikeys, a whole new design for living a life! A life that starts with the end.

Now, when I say "the end," I don't mean THE end! I mean, it's advisable to have a solid will and make some preparations for when your life ends, but that's not what I'm talking about here.

Let's pick something, something fairly innocuous and random. Your income. Are you happy with where you are financially? Do you feel as if you could accomplish more in this area of your life? Perhaps this is an area where you have been self-sabotaging!

Okay, let's *Star Trek* the shit outta this thing! Start with the end.

Look ahead from this very moment. Let your imagination run a little to a year ahead, maybe two. What will your financial future look like then? Doubled your income? $10,000 in savings?

This isn't the same as making goals or visualizing or manifesting, by the way. This is about creating your future and powerfully dealing with everything that comes up either as an obstacle or constraint or your typical self-sabotaging bullshittery. You're being pulled toward that future. Not struggling to get there.

You chip away at and deal with anything that isn't that future. And you love it. Why? Because for once in your life, you are the architect and the artist. You don't need to be a warrior or a fighter. You become a creator, someone who thinks from the future, a visionary of your own making.

This is about designing the life you want. The kind of life that inspires you and lifts you up. A complete redirection from your self-sabotaging ways.

Michelangelo, the Italian sculptor, painter, architect, and poet of the High Renaissance, had an unparalleled influence on the development of Western art and is considered by some to be one of the greatest artists of all time.

One of his greatest works was the seventeen-foot-high, six-ton statue *David*, hewn from a solid block of pristine Italian Carrara marble. It has been said that

Michelangelo did not make the statue in the way you or I might think he did. Rather, he removed everything from that block that was not *David*. It seems, in Michelangelo's mind, *David* was already complete, only waiting to be revealed, piece by piece by piece. He used two years of his life, fully invested in that passion, uncovering the future from the present.

He sculpted from the future to the present until that future was realized. Then he filled his life with the next future and the next future and the next future. Every day he was a sculptor. He wasn't trying to become one someday. He filled his life with the problems a sculptor would have and gave himself fully to them. And the work? Lit. Him. Up.

Try on the idea that until now, you have been hacking at that giant rock called your life with no real creativity or genius, no future to inspire the present, nothing to call you to be a greater self. Instead, you've been making a series of random swings at the mass in front of you to live in the hope that you'll make something worthwhile out of it. Eventually.

This book has never been about goals or success in the typical way you have thought about it. That way of living has you sacrifice your hours, days, and weeks on this earth for a fleeting moment of satisfaction or accomplishment "someday," trying to get somewhere but never really being "here." The flashes of success that do come your way are quickly forgotten or shelved because you have nothing in your life to call you to greatness!

For once, this is about populating your *current* life with the kind of purpose and activity that invigorates you. A life of your design, one that compels you to act in new ways on the things that matter to you most! A life that each and every day you are working on, chipping away at that giant block of stone, constantly revealing and uncovering the kind of future you once thought beyond your reach. Every day you are either going to work to make a living or you are revealing a future you never thought possible!

I couldn't care less about what you think you *can* do! What about a life blossoming daily in a constant season under the gratifying labor of what you think you *cannot* do? A life where you enliven yourself by reaching for the stars every single day. Whatever your version of that might be. Listen, you'll never get rid of problems in your life, but you could start engaging with the kind of problems Michelangelo did, the problems that make a life worthwhile and satisfying. Not eventually either. The kind of life that inspires you *today*.

> "... A thing constructed can only be loved after it is constructed; but a thing created is loved before it exists."
> —*Charles Dickens*

Why did I become a writer? Because I wanted to live that life. All of it. I didn't have an aim of *becoming* a writer. It wasn't a goal or something I was out to get better at or improve until I could wear the badge with honor. I *started* with being a writer and built a life that could make that work. I filled my life with the problems that a writer would have. I became invigorated and enlivened by the challenge of what that demanded of me and how to solve the issues that presented themselves when I took on the notion that who I *am* is a writer. FUCK!! SUDDENLY I WAS A WRITER!

The same philosophy applies in every area of your life. Is your marriage about just getting along or could it be about authentic, passionate love in new and expanding ways? One will challenge you to discover new ways to express yourself, reveal your limitations, and fill your life with the challenges of a special kind of life, and the other won't. Both will give rise to obstacles and issues. One will enliven; the other will slowly kill your relationship.

Are you saving money to improve your credit, or are you revealing a new future of complete financial freedom? One will inspire new actions and creativity; the other will dull your senses.

What about your body? Are you eating to lose weight, or are you revealing an entirely new approach to living an unrecognizable, healthy life of your own creation?

In each of these cases, you would be confronted with the kinds of actions that would require you to stretch and reach for something greater. It wouldn't necessarily be comfortable, but it would be a discomfort of your own creation, and each moment of pain or unease would be another chip away at revealing the future that you designed.

In each and every moment of your life, you will be faced with a choice. The choice either to be guided by the past you had no say in or to be called out by the future you created. Uncovering your self-sabotage mechanism here has now put your hands on the levers and dials of that choice. It's yours to make.

What actions are you taking today that align you with a new future? What are you chipping away at that reveals your work, your dreams, your passions, or your purpose? What lights you up? What masterpieces could you reveal?

In short, what are you actually up to that would make this life of yours a truly great one?

13

You Can Finally Stop Doing That Shit— No, Really!

You're not broken, there's nothing to fix. You're not a fucking chair, you're an expression, so get out there and express your future. Make it something great, something worth giving your life to. Everything else is just complaining and shit coffee.

The beautiful thing about this future-oriented approach is that the future is truly unlimited. I mean, there's nothing formed out there, so you can do what you want with it. It's expansive and can include anything. When you leave the past where it sleeps, when you're no longer framing what's in front of you in terms of what's behind you, you really have limitless potential.

As long as you stay aware.

Your future might look like having a better and more prestigious career. Or maybe starting your own business. Or founding a charity. Or being financially viable or in the relationship you always wanted. Perhaps you'll find the freedom to work from where you want, whether it's a home office or a café in a foreign country. Or you'll make your creative idea finally go viral.

In your future you might run marathons, write a novel, or be conversational in a new language. Your body might look a certain way, or your friendships might be rich and vibrant. It's all about your vision. Everything else is just old brain patterns and behaviors.

Remember, this is not about stopping self-sabotaging behaviors on their own but instead designing a future that compels you to fill your life with new actions, new outcomes—in short, a new life. And you can have it now. Right now.

"But, but, but, GARY!!!!! I don't know what to do with my life!"

Bullshit! That's yet another excuse to keep you tied to the past. It might not seem like an excuse to you, but it is. It doesn't matter *what* you do; it only matters *that* you do. You can't find the pathway there by standing still. Life is nothing but a grand experiment, an opening in a moment in history to shout, scream, love, live, and die, but you won't do that by sitting on your ass worrying about the *right* thing to do with your life. A tremendous amount of amazing discoveries were made by accident, not by plan. Try something, and if it doesn't work, try something else! That's the beauty of this. It's an exploration of what it is to be alive.

> *Every day, several times a day, sometimes hundreds of times a day and for countless days to come, you have to ask yourself, "What is my future telling me to do right now?"*

Whatever the answer is, big or small, ACT ON IT!

I need to stop you here. I've just given you the keys to the fucking kingdom. Everything you ever wanted, just waiting to be chipped at. Should there be doubts? Yes. Might you get a bit scared or confused? Yep. What about those old patterns; are they coming back?

Yes, they are. "My self-defeating dialogue will still be there?" Uh-huh. "My fear of being rejected?" Yes. "The weight of the struggle of life?" Yes.

Yes, yes, yes, yes, fucking yes. And so what?

We've just torn your past a new one in these pages. We've dug deep, gone right into the face of your most negative, most disparaging self. In the beginning of the book, I said we were going to work on uncovering and transforming the bullshit that constantly sabotages your life. By now, you should be familiar with all of those thoughts, those emotions, those intimate and habitual behaviors and feelings that are unique to how you experience life and that crop up when you're sabotaging your life.

If you're not profoundly connected to all of the ways in which you have systematically sabotaged yourself, go back and connect with the life you were thrown into, see if you can uncover your established truths that led to the three saboteurs, and get in touch with that familiar point of experience from which you start every day. Read this again as many times as you need to and with a different pair of eyes each time. The eyes that are actually looking to change your life.

Martin Heidegger believed that once we understand the ways we're thrown, our whole life opens up. Until that point, our thrown-ness defines who we are, but once we've uncovered the way it works, we find true freedom. We're able to surpass it in a way, to go beyond it and explore what it is to be a human being.

But that requires one important attribute. Ownership. Whatever you own no longer owns you. That's why we have done all this work, dug in as deep as we have: for you to define and make clear whatever has had you be on autopilot. To wake you up. To make you aware.

Good! Now you're finally aware!

And now you have to take responsibility for all that you are now aware of. You don't get to use the same tired excuses, the same old moments of self-indulged guilt or shame or weakness. Sure, there will be moments, real in-your-face moments when the compulsion to do the predictable will be so enticing, so magnetic and powerful, the urge will seem like it's just too much.

For example, maybe you are finally committed to ending the cycle of sabotaging your marriage and instead you are working to reveal a connection of love and adventure in your relationship. But what do you do when your partner says that thing, you know the thing, the one that you completely lose your shit when they say it? In that moment you have to stop and choose. Remember that future you created, the one that is a symbol of the life and relationship you have always wanted, and start chipping. You chip,

chip away in that moment. You remove the obstacle. You don't fight it, you don't hate it or get dramatic about it, saying something that will hurt your partner and your connection. You move it to the side and let it pass through, unperturbed, and you take the action in that moment that is in alignment with that future of love and adventure. Authentically pivot.

That action might look like apologizing, or telling your partner you love them, or asking for a minute to gather yourself. These types of actions are an interruption to the drive of the compulsion to self-sabotage and an example of the relationship of love and adventure you are after.

And then it's gone. Until the next time.

And then the next time, you move it to the side again, replacing it again with an action that makes that loving marriage you are after more real, more present in the moment. And you'll do this every time because that's what someone does when their very existence is about having love in their life. They bring it to the table.

You might have to do this two times a day, you might have to do this two hundred times a day. You see, that's what it takes to make real and lasting change. Commitment. Real, no-kidding, all-in, nothing-left-out commitment to what you really want. Especially in those moments when you are defeated or depressed or confused or any one of the number of ways in which you find an excuse to bail on yourself.

Then there will be those days when you blow it. That's right, you might blow it, but even then, in the aftermath of *that*, you look to the future for guidance on how to clean it up. If you're committed to love and adventure in your relationship and you've just blown it by saying the not-so-safe word that you're not supposed to say in a moment of upset, what does love and adventure now demand of you? Take ownership, apologize, and move on into that loving and adventurous relationship that you created in your future.

It doesn't matter if you blow it. What matters is that you keep working on the stone, creating and chipping away at your own masterpiece. That you honor the future you created.

Michelangelo already had *David* in his mind, remember? All he did was reveal the future he had created, and that's all you have to do here, REVEAL THE FUTURE, every day, one piece at a time. You don't seriously think he didn't have to fix some self-imposed messes along the way, do you?

The same old stuff will occasionally get in the way for you too. It'll rise up and slap you around the head.

That's when who you could be becomes more important than who you were.

NO LONGER SHAPED BY THE PAST
BUT INSTEAD INFORMED BY THE FUTURE

All of the shit that I showed you, dragged you through, and made you face in this book has led to this, your real opportunity for change. Not the fake stuff you were attempting in the past, trying to fix a broken reality. This is the real, deep, fundamental change, change that's based on an entirely new set of rules and way of doing things.

This isn't about a single future either. This isn't some feathery, vague dream of a future but rather a myriad of futures. A life that's peppered with the future of your finances, your love life, your family, your body, your career or business or purpose for this life.

You need to define that future for all of these things. Where are you headed? What will your life really look like in two or three or five years? What are you creating? Are you going to sit there and throw that up to fate, or will you define it for yourself and challenge yourself to live that reality, moment by moment by moment?

What have you been killing off or waiting for or screwing around with? Start getting up to the sort of stuff that inspires you!

Right now, start creating this future life in your mind's eye, including all the different things you'd like to see in it and who you could be in it. Imagine the kind of work you'll do a year from now. What actions are you taking today to reveal that future? What kind of relationship do you want to have? Can you see it? All right, now look at this present moment of time. What actions are you taking right now to reveal *that* future?

It goes on. Picture where you'll live, in what kind of house and in what location—no, really, get specific. Picture who will share it with you, whether it's a lover, your family, or your dogs, or maybe you'll be on your own! Now, take a look at your current life next to all of that. Your current life is the block of stone, the future is your *David*. What do you need to work on first? What will you be challenged by? Maybe you need to end a sterile relationship or take on some other big piece of your life. I get it. It won't be easy, but remember, you are going to live either a life of regurgitating the past or a life of revealing a whole new future . . . it's time to choose.

There's no magical secret to your life, no single potion, no mystical source to your stuff, no one thing that can turn you into your greatest self or gushing with new-age purpose.

You're more like a body of work than a body, and there's always work to do, new levels of

*effectiveness and aliveness to
unpack and explore. And every day
of your life, either you're getting
yourself on the hook for that task or
you're dead in the water. Period.*

The universe doesn't have your back, your front, your top, or your bottom, and things happen only for the reason you give them. That's it.

Stop indulging yourself with fantasies and dramas and unresolved issues. Wake the hell up!

Every experience you have, from anger to depression to joy, excitement, and apathy, they're all human, but you don't have to jump into bed with them every time they show up in your head!

They're all appropriate to the human experience; just don't get hooked on any one of them! You're not broken, there's nothing to fix. You're not a fucking chair, you're an expression, so get out there and express your future. Make it something great, something worth giving your life to.

Do you know what life *really* is? It's an opportunity for you to play with the skinbag you were given. To try it out, to take it for a ride, to work that thing to its very limit, to live this life before you fucking die. The certainty you've been craving? That's it right there. You'll die.

Between now and then, you have this glorious opportunity to go beyond everything you've ever known yourself as. To be the most effective, loving, forgiving, adventurous, passionate, committed, understanding, successful, and creative human being you can muster until you're out of time. To look the people in your life straight in the eye and be the kind of human being you've always wanted to be. Authentic.

Everything else is just complaining and shit coffee.

If you're not inspired by your life, you haven't created one worthy enough to light you up, and that, my magic little sponge, is always on you. When it comes down to it, do you know why you self-sabotage? You're bored. You're bored out of your freaking mind by your own predictable, safe, ordinary little bathtub of bullshit. You know it and I know it. I don't care how many certificates or diplomas you have, how much money is in your bank account, or the size of your Twitter following. Your life has become a mundane and repetitive attempt at wrestling yourself free from a past that you decided you'd never be able to get over anyway. It's completely mental.

Fuck the past, reveal a bold future, step out there and get into action. Deal with yourself.

Own your life, own where it's been, own where it's headed and what you need to do to wake yourself up to what's possible each and every day of it.

The future has arrived. Now, what the hell are you going to do about it?

About the Author

Born and raised in Glasgow, Scotland, Gary John Bishop moved to the United States in 1997. This opened up his pathway to the world of personal development, specifically to his love of ontology and phenomenology. This approach, in which he rigorously trained for a number of years, saw him rise to become a senior program director with one of the world's leading personal development companies. After years of facilitating programs for thousands of people all over the world and later studying and being influenced by the philosophies of Martin Heidegger, Hans-Georg Gadamer, and Edmund Husserl, Gary is producing his own brand of "urban philosophy." His lifelong commitment to shifting people's ability to exert real change in their lives drives him each and every day. He has a no-frills, no-bullshit approach that has brought him an ever-increasing following, drawn to the simplicity and real-world use of his work.